CULTURE SHOCK!
SHOCK!

Nepal

WITHDRAWN

Jon Burbank

Graphic Arts Center Publishing Company
Portland, Oregon

Illustrations by TRIGG
Photographs by Jon Burbank
Cover photographs by Jon Burbank

© 1992 Times Editions Pte Ltd

This book is published by special
arrangement with Times Editions Pte Ltd
International Standard Book Number 1-55868-076-4
Library of Congress Catalog Number 91-074107
Graphic Arts Center Publishing Company
P.O. Box 10306 • Portland, Oregon 97210 • (503) 226-2402

Printed in Singapore by Chong Moh Offset Printing Pte Ltd

CONTENTS

PREFACE

This book aims to help both the short term tourist and the expatriate enjoy their time in Nepal. These are two very different groups, but anyone spending more than a few days in Nepal will find their interests sometimes fall into 'the other group's' concern.

Nepal is a collage of cultures, with some aspects differing as much from each other as they do with us. This book discusses the most commonly held beliefs and the major differences between groups. It covers most of the basic situations and problems encountered in Nepal by both tourists and expatriates. It also tries to give some background information on why things are the way they are.

Most people fall in love with Nepal. Many go to great lengths scheming and scamming to stay or come back. But some people are on the first plane back out again or spend their entire time shutting themselves in their own tiny cultural ghetto. Nepal is a very strong experience, with life's enchantment and beauty side by side with its ugliness and despair on any street or trail.

You can make your adjustment quicker and easier by doing some careful mental packing before you come. Pack your patience, tolerance, flexibility, curiosity, and of course, your sense of humor. You'll find they make your adjustment easier (and make it easier for people to adjust to you).

Leave behind your rose-colored glasses – you're not going to Shangri-La, no matter what Nepal's tourist literature may tell you. Leave behind your expectations, too. Don't go expecting spiritual revelation or expecting to bring prosperity to Nepal's people. It's not going to happen. That doesn't mean leave behind your goals, drive, energy, ambition, and joy in new experiences; just don't bring expectations – there's a difference.

Ke garne translates as 'what to do'. Nepalis use it on any occasion things are not as they should be. It's sometimes said as a request for help or guidance, an excuse, an angry demand for action, or a laughing comment on life's absurdity. You'll hear it everywhere and probably catch yourself using it soon after you arrive.

I think this book will answer most of your questions, but I'll give you a good example of how to use 'ke garne' right now. In anticipation of any answers not found in this book, ke garne? I apologize, but with a country as diverse as Nepal, no book can have all the answers. I do hope, though, this book can at least make you comfortable in Nepal and open some doors for you.

Don't be shy about asking Nepalis questions. There are few places where culture is such a favorite topic of conversation. Nepalis genuinely enjoy discussing their culture, so take advantage of their curiosity to satisfy your own.

I did, and I'd like to finish by thanking Nepal and all my friends there for their years of friendship, kindness, and patience. I hope I can continue to go back and benefit from Nepal for years to come.

Jon Burbank
July 1991

– Chapter One –

THE MOUNTAIN KINGDOM

THE GEOGRAPHY OF NEPAL

The founder of modern Nepal, King Prithvi Narayan Shah, referred to the country as a yam stuck between two boulders. The two boulders are India and China. The two most populous countries in the world and the traditional giants of the Asian mainland, they surround Nepal on all four sides, keeping it locked into the Himalayan mountains and away from the ocean.

There are few places in the world where geography is such a dominant factor in the life and character of the people. Everything from tropical jungles to arctic tundras are scrunched into an area the size of the states of New York and Connecticut combined.

In about 160 kilometers (100 miles) as the crow flies, Nepal's altitude changes from about 200 m (658 ft) in the south to over 8,848 m (29,028 ft) on the peak of Mt Everest, the world's highest mountain, in the north.

Mountains cover 80% of Nepal. Flying over them you see people living wherever they can. You see cascades of terraces with scarcely a tree in sight. In the dry season the slopes are faded brown and look like dry skin, but in the monsoon they're an iridescent emerald green with rice and corn.

Mountains and terraces may be beautiful to look at; but try living there, farming there. Try building a road across and you'll realize why Nepal remains one of the poorest and most under-developed countries in the world. The scarcity of resources makes developing any industry almost impossible. Over 90% of the population depends on farming, and even that is at subsistence level at best.

The Monsoon: Blessing and Curse

If mountains dominate the landscape, the monsoon dominates the weather. The monsoon comes in mid-June every year, and Nepali farmers know they can rely on it.

With almost no irrigation, Nepali farmers depend on the regular rains from mid-June to mid-September to provide the large amounts of water they need for their rice, corn, and wheat crops.

The monsoon rains are Nepal's boon, but they're a mixed bless-ing. In the early 1980s a not uncommon tragedy struck. A downpour caused a landslide on a steep slope. The landslide formed a natural mud dam across the river at the base of the hill. While a riverside bazaar slept, the downpour continued and a lake built up behind the dam. In the middle of the night the dam finally broke. Tons of water and mud swept downstream, wiping out the sleeping bazaar and killing over a hundred people. Nepal's farmers have good reason for their stoicism and acceptance of fate.

Water and Development

As soon as development experts crossed Nepal's mountains in the 1950s, they touted the hundreds of rivers flowing between those mountains as Nepal's greatest resource and potential money earner.

Experts estimated Nepal has 83,000 megawatts of hydroelectric potential, which may be the highest per capita potential in the world. Dam the rivers, build hydroelectric plants, use what electricity you need, then sell the rest, they said.

As with most development schemes, the realities of the country mocked the ideas of the experts. Forty years after development efforts started, most of Nepal's population remains without electricity. Where there is electricity, it is usually a 20 or 40 watt bulb in the room, with a wood fire cooking the food under it.

The huge Kulekani power station was supposed to end Kathmandu's power rationing when it became operational in 1982. By 1987 there was rationing again as sporadic monsoon rains failed to provide enough water to fill the reservoir.

Several large projects are in various stages of execution. The uncertainties of Nepal's young geology, the difficulty of constructing not only the dam but the massive infrastructure to make dam construction possible, the high cost of the foreign machinery and technology needed to produce the electricity have all made the cost of producing electricity much higher than was originally thought.

Nepal's geography makes it one of the most beautiful and thrilling places in the world to visit, and one of the most daunting to live in. It is a dominant force in shaping the life and character of the people. Studying Nepal's geography will help you understand its people as well.

Stripes

Nepal looks like someone took a map, crumpled it up and then didn't even try to smooth it out again. If you look past all the crinkles, though, you will see that Nepal is actually a series of

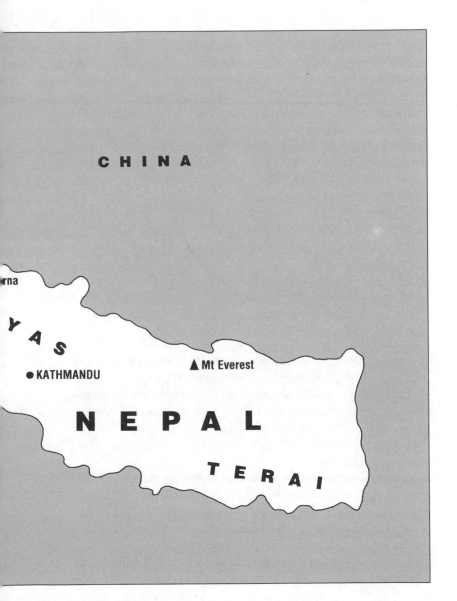

stripes running east to west across the country.

All along the northern border run the Himalayas, the highest mountains in the world. Below them is a broad band of peaks called the Mahabharat or the Middle Hills. The Mahabharat hills can rise as high as 2,800 m (9,214 ft), with steep river valleys running through them at less than 600 m (1,975 ft) elevation.

Below the Mahabharat comes the only flat area in Nepal. Called the Terai, it can be subdivided into three sections.

Directly south of the Mahabharat comes the inner Terai, also called the 'Dun'. The Dun is actually a string of low valleys running east to west. Their elevation is usually well below 500 m (1,645 ft).

South of the inner Terai is a narrow band of low hills (low in the Nepali context) called the Siwalik Hills, with a maximum height of about 1,500 m (4,936 ft).

Finally, along the southern border with India is a 25–40 kilometer (15.5–24.8 mile) strip that is the true Terai. This is the only truly flat area in the country.

The Himalayas

The name 'Himalaya' comes from the Sanskrit words *hima* meaning 'snow', and *alaya* meaning 'dwelling place'.

Mt Everest's traditional names are Sagarmatha on the Nepali side and Chomolungma on the Tibetan side, both meaning 'mother of the earth'. Across the border in Tibet near Humla is Mt Kailash, the home of the great god Shiva to the Hindus and the center of the universe to Tibetans.

In central Nepal sits a huge group of mountains that are certainly some of the best rain catchers in the world. Lumle, at their base, is one of the wettest places in Nepal, with about 565 cm (222 inches) of rain per year. The grateful farmers who live below this massif named it Annapurna, the goddess of grains.

The Himalayas stretch all across the northern border of Nepal. At altitudes of over 3,000 meters (about 10,000 ft), the Himalayan

A typical scene in the Middle Hills. Rows of ridges end in the massive Himalayan mountains. Villages stride the ridge tops with terraces running all the way down to rivers below. Himalayan villages lie behind these peaks.

zone makes up over 25% of Nepal's land area. The youth of the mountains can be seen in their steep slopes and jagged profiles. There are few real valleys, and most rivers run through steep gorges.

Winter days in the thinner air of the mountains can be blazing hot, but temperatures quickly drop below freezing at sunset. The monsoon's effect is determined by the local formation of the mountains, but in general the monsoon rains are cut off by the high peaks.

There are eight peaks over 8,000 m (26,326 ft): Everest, Kanchenjunga, Lhotse, Makalu, Cho Oyu, Dhaulagiri, Manaslu, and Annapurna.

About 10% of Nepal's population live in this high area. Cultivation is possible up to about 4,200 m (13,821 ft). The main crops are potato, millet, and barley, but it is impossible to survive on the food that can be scraped out of high altitude fields.

People who live in this area are mostly semi-nomadic, keeping large herds of sheep and yaks, using summer pastures at up to 5,000 m (16,454 ft). People also spend months on the road with herds of sheep or trading between southern Nepal and Tibet in the north. In western Nepal men, sometimes whole families, migrate to India and spend the winter there as day laborers.

The Middle Hills

This is Nepal's heartland. Large migration to the recently-opened Terai means the Middle Hills no longer hold the majority of the population, but about 40% of Nepal still live on these steep-sided hills. The vast majority of those who have moved down to the Terai will still name their old home in the hills when you ask where they come from.

Nepal is not just divided into east-west stripes. Each of those stripes is fragmented into hundreds of ridges, as if someone has dropped bands of colored glass on the floor and just threw the same color pieces back together, making no attempt to fit the pieces to each other.

In the east, the hills are jammed close together and the slopes are very steep. The monsoon rains are plentiful and regular. The regularity of the rains is good for growing crops, but the steepness of the slopes makes farming extremely difficult.

The east is by no means rich, but compared to western Nepal it is prosperous. There are more ethnic groups here, and the different communities are more integrated than groups in the west, physically if not socially.

There are more schools, medical services, and development projects available in the east, but, again, that's measured against western Nepal. Schools and medical services are still very inadequate; there are no roads, electricity, or industry. This is still the fifth world, one of the poorest countries on the globe.

Farther west, the land becomes drier. Traveling to the west from the east, you will feel like you have left the monsoon behind, even though local people will still complain about the heavy rains.

The landscape, while still not flat, is more open; the sides of valleys are farther apart, and the landscape is on a bigger scale. In the east you feel you could shout to a friend on the other side of the valley. In the west you are lucky to see a moving speck across the valley.

The regions inhabited by Nepal's tribal groups end at the Kali Gandaki in the center of the country. To the west, caste Hindu Brahmins and Chhetris predominate. According to Dor Bahadur Bista's *People of Nepal*, they make up over 80% of the people who live in this region.

The western Mahabharat is noticeably poorer than the east. Travelers to the area know how difficult it can be to find food and shelter, particularly in the pre-monsoon dry months when food stocks are especially low.

Schools are few and far between and there are few female children in this more conservative area getting any kind of education. The nearest road or airport may be a week's walk away.

The Terai

The Terai is the northern limit of the enormous flood plain of the Ganges River, the great holy river of the Hindu religion, about 200 kilometers (124 miles) to the south.

Until the mid-1950s, a journey through the Terai, particularly the valleys of the inner Terai, was a desperate rush through dense jungle full of tigers, rhinoceroses, elephants, cobras and other poisonous snakes, and scorpions. Most dreaded were the thick, buzzing clouds of mosquitoes carrying a particularly severe form of malaria, the dreaded *aul*.

The only people who lived in the Terai's forbidding jungles were small tribal groups like the Tharus, who had developed a

The Terai is the only place in Nepal with long, flat vistas. The region has become the nation's breadbasket and will soon hold more than 50% of the population even though it makes up only about 15% of the land area.

natural immunity to malaria.

The Nepalis always knew that the Terai, with its flat landscape and fertile soil, had economic potential; the problem was developing it. Traditionally the government of Nepal granted lands in the Terai to its high generals and officials, who ruled like feudal lords and gave a share of their harvest to the king.

Development of the Terai, mainly its agriculture and timber, happened slowly. It was not until the World Health Organization started spraying the mosquitoes (with DDT) in the 1950s that the area really opened up.

The government offered numerous incentives to hill people and many families have moved down. At the same time thousands of Indians moved across the border to take advantage of the better opportunities available in Nepal.

This southern border with India is basically an open one. It is marked only by a series of concrete pillars in most places, and these pillars wander back and forth sometimes. There is no system of passport checks. Nepal has tried to implement a system of identity cards or working papers for Indian citizens in Nepal, but the Indian government has bitterly opposed this.

Today the Terai is Nepal's fastest growing area. Fifty percent of Nepal's population live in the Terai and this percentage continues to grow. The Terai is Nepal's breadbasket (and ricebowl) and its industrial center as well.

However, problems continue to arise between the Nepali and Indian segments of the population, mainly over job and land rights.

Traditionally the Terai has been administered from the capital, Kathmandu, by bureaucrats whose viewpoint is that of the Middle Hills. As vital as the Terai is to Nepal, its views and needs have neither been asked nor considered commensurate with its importance.

As the Terai's portion of Nepal's population and economic output continues to grow, and with the implementation of a truly democratic government, the region's voice in the country's government and policy-making should grow dramatically. When Nepal becomes a true democracy, the seat of government will stay in the hills, but the real power will sit in the Terai.

HISTORY

A long time ago, the Kathmandu Valley was a turquoise-blue lake. The great holy man Vipaswi Buddha came and sat on the hill of Nagarjun, taking advantage of its beauty and calm to meditate. Gladdened by his contemplation, he planted a lotus seed in the lake. On the full moon six months later a lotus emerged and opened, filling the valley with the glow of a blue flame containing the image of Swayambhu, 'the self-existent one'.

As the luminescence rose to the heavens, the holy warrior Manjushri in far-off Tibet saw it and resolved to find it. He stopped on the hill top of Nagarkot and meditated on Lord Swayambhu's radiance three days and nights. To worship more closely, Manjushri walked to the southern rim of the valley. Rushing down from Pulchowk, with one stroke of his sword, he cut the gorge at Chobar that still drains Kathmandu. The heavenly lotus settled on the hill of Swayambhu, where Manjushri built a shrine.

That's the story of the valley's founding, and it actually was a lake thousands of years ago. But we have to wait until about the 7th century B.C. and the arrival of the Kiratis (or Kirantis) for the start of recorded settlement.

The Kiratis

The Kirati tribe, probably of Mongolian origin, came out of the east to establish a powerful kingdom in the valley. The Kiratis were fine warriors. Yalambar, the first and greatest of their 29 kings, fought and died in the climactic battle of the *Mahabharata* (one of the two great epics of the Hindu religion).

The Kirati kingdom founded many of the valley's settlements

and monuments. Being Hindus, they worshiped Shiva. Large quantities of Nepali wool were sold in the then great city of Pataliputra (today's Patna) and trade was conducted as far away as Sri Lanka and Tibet.

The great Indian emperor Ashok is said to have visited the valley during the 3rd century B.C., erecting Patan's four stupas. His daughter Charumati married a valley prince, Devapala, and together they founded a beautiful town, Deopatan, near today's Chabil.

The Licchavis drove out the Kiratis in about A.D. 300. The Kiratis resettled in their eastern homeland, the forebears of today's Rais and Limbus.

The Licchavis

The Licchavis were Rajputs driven from their kingdom in North India. Their rule was one of Nepal's golden ages. Trade between India and China made the kingdom prosper.

Licchavi Nepal reached its zenith under Amshuvaraman. His beautiful seven-story palace in Deopatan, Kailashkut Bhavan, was legendary. He sponsored poets and himself wrote a book of grammar. He also managed to resist pressure from both India and Tibet, marrying his sister to an Indian prince and his daughter to Tibet's powerful king.

Rule of Nepal passed to Thakuri kings from Nuwakot as Nepal slipped into its 'dark ages' (the late 7th century to the 13th century). The valley was invaded (unsuccessfully) by Tibet in 705 and by Kashmir in 782. Records are sketchy, but many institutions of modern Nepal were founded at that time, including the cult of the living goddess, the Kumari.

King Gunakamadeva stands out during this period. He is credited with founding Kathmandu (called Kirtipur then) and building Kasthamandap, the temple which Kathmandu takes its name from, with the wood of a single tree. Indra Jatra, the greatest festival of the valley, is also said to have started during his reign.

The Mallas

The Mallas were forced out of India in about 1200 after a long history of ruling there. Their name is found both in the *Mahabharata* and in Buddhist literature. These sources show them ruling small kingdoms as far back as 600 B.C.

Initially the Malla period was a continuation of the violence and destruction of the dark ages. Raiders from Mithila, a North Indian kingdom, plundered the valley five times between 1244 and 1311, when they razed Patan. Worse, a horrendous earthquake in 1245 destroyed the entire valley, killing a third of the population.

Kathmandu has always been the center of Nepal, but as the Mallas tried to establish themselves in the valley, the Khas kingdom in western Nepal rose to become their only serious rival.

Today little is known of this kingdom centered around Sinja in the Jumla area, but Khasa raiders put prolonged pressure on Kathmandu's Mallas, striking the valley six times between 1287 and 1344. The Khas could never sustain any momentum, though, and their raids, like their kingdom, faded away.

In 1346 an army under Sultan Shamsuddin of Bengal ravaged the valley for a week. It took the Mallas decades to reassert social and political order.

Shamsuddin's attack was only one example of the waves of Moslems sweeping across India, breaking up the Hindu kingdoms. Some of this Hindu aristocracy fled into Nepal's hills to form dozens of hilltop kingdoms: the *baaisi raja* (22 kingdoms) of west Nepal and the *chaubisi raja* (24 kingdoms) of central Nepal.

The Moslem conquests forced the migration of waves of Hindus to the Middle Hills, particularly in the west. These migrations established the population profile that exists to this day.

One family, the Shahs, set up a small kingdom around its hilltop palace in Gorkha after fleeing from Rajastan; they came perhaps from Udaipur, in 1303. Four centuries later they conquered the Kathmandu Valley.

From this hilltop palace in Gorkha, King Prithvi Narayan Shah set out and established modern Nepal when he conquered and unified the Kathmandu Valley.

The Shahs

Prithvi Narayan Shah coveted the valley even before he became king of Gorkha in 1742. By 1745 he gained his first victory (after his first defeat), capturing Nuwakot northwest of the valley.

It took him 23 long years and several defeats, but he finally did it, making his triumphant entry on the main day of the Indra Jatra festival in 1768.

A strong nationalist, he was determined to preserve and protect his kingdom and its lucrative trade position. Foreigners and missionaries were not allowed into the country, and Nepal followed this policy of isolation until 1951.

His successors expanded the kingdom till it reached Kashmir and Tibet, and included Sikkim in the east. An attempt to expand into Tibet led to a disastrous war.

The Gorkhali system of rewarding soldiers and officers with tracts of land (in lieu of pay) necessitated expansion, and the Terai was the only place to go. Nepal quickly came in conflict with the

other expanding power in the area: the British East India Company.

The British

In 1810 the two powers went to war. After some initial successes, the Nepalis were forced to settle when a British army threatened to invade Kathmandu. Under the 1816 Treaty of Friendship negotiated at Sigauli, Nepal lost all territory to the east and west of its present borders and most of the Terai.

In addition, the British gained the right to station a 'resident' in Kathmandu. But the Nepalis got the last word in: the resident was given the worst piece of land they could find and he was forbidden from traveling outside the boundaries of the Kathmandu Valley.

A Crisis

With external expansion impossible, Nepal's leaders found enemies among themselves. The king deliberately kept his chain of command unclear, the queen schemed on her own. The court became a maze of plots and intrigues. One night, after the murder of the queen's lover, fighting broke out in the palace.

Jang Bahadur Rana (a main figure in the palace intrigues), who had the foresight to bring not only his brothers but his troops as well, made the most of the opportunity.

The 'Kot Massacre' determined the course of Nepal's history for more than the next 100 years. Jang Bahadur declared himself prime minister. The king and queen, once his patrons, now did as he said: the royal family became mere figureheads.

Rana family life was dominated by its own internal intrigues and squabbles as brothers and cousins plotted to grab power from each other, but until 1951 they ruled Nepal as their own private estate.

The Ranas

Importing marble floors and crystal chandeliers from Europe, the Ranas built enormous palaces in a mishmash of European styles while the rest of the country stayed frozen in the Middle Ages. Today the Ranas' gaudy palaces are government offices and hotels, the only reminders of their century of rule.

The Ranas were not interested in anything that did not directly benefit them. Anything that could lead to opposition, education for example, was suppressed. In 1952 only 10% of the population was considered literate.

Opposition and protest were ruthlessly suppressed. Exposed to the outside world through their military service, returning Gurkha soldiers were one of the first groups to voice objections, founding the Gurkha League, a semi-political organization, in 1921.

The first open protest against the Ranas was a strike at a jute mill in Biratnagar on March 4, 1947. The strike was led by B.P. Koirala, the charismatic president of the Nepali National Congress (NNC) formed in India in 1946.

The Ranas had always depended on the strong patronage of the British, whom they supported in peace and war with Gurkha soldiers. Newly-independent India pressed the British to stop influencing Nepal (and in effect established its own claim to that right).

The Ranas tried to widen their base by ending Nepal's diplomatic isolation, instituting a constitution, and signing a treaty with India recognizing Nepal's sovereignty and independence.

The Shahs Again

But opposition led by the NNC and B.P. Koirala scoffed at the 'reforms' and opposition became more widespread and vocal. The Ranas were shaken, but refused to let go.

The figurehead king, Tribuvan, was the catalyst that led to the Ranas' downfall. On November 6, 1950, he left the palace on a family outing. As his guards watched in shock, the royal family's cars suddenly veered and roared the short distance into the Indian Embassy where he requested asylum.

His guards were not the only ones shocked: the Ranas, the NNC,

India, Britain – everyone was caught by surprise. Tribuvan was allowed to fly to India. The NNC, not wanting to lose initiative to the king, took control of Birgunj and, by January 1951, controlled the Terai.

The Ranas' days were over. An interim government, half Rana-half NNC, was formed, and on February 18, 1951, Tribuvan returned as king promising a transition to democracy.

Democracy proved difficult to bring about, though. Tribuvan died in 1955 and his son, Mahendra, finally oversaw the first general election in Nepal's history in February and March of 1959.

B.P. Koirala became the new prime minister and his new party, the Nepal Congress Party (NCP), controlled a strong majority. The parliament was as boisterous as any new democracy's will be and there were charges that some were using democracy to line their own pockets. Mahendra, a strong personality, grew impatient as his own policies were slighted and his position ignored.

At noon, on December 15, 1960, Mahendra sent army officers to arrest the cabinet. The country was in chaos, he said, brought on by democracy, a foreign idea inappropriate to Nepal. He took direct control. Political parties were banned, B.P. Koirala spent the next 20 years in jail and exile.

Mahendra instituted the 'panchayat' system, with a prime minister and cabinet appointed and dismissed directly by the king. Criticizing the monarchy became a criminal offense, and freedom of assembly, speech and the press was sharply cut.

Birendra, the current king, succeeded Mahendra in 1972 and declared his intention of maintaining the status quo. But returning soldiers and students, improved communication, and increased education made Nepalis more aware of their impoverished situation.

It was impossible to hide corruption that seemed to grow in direct proportion to the large amounts of development aid coming in. People began demanding more accountability or at least a bigger share of the pie.

A Long Time Coming

In 1979 protests erupted in the streets. Violent demonstrations shook Kathmandu until Birendra announced he would consent to a referendum on whether to allow political parties. B.P. Koirala, much older and frailer now, was allowed to campaign. The panchayat system won a slim majority.

Even before the vote, the king made further reforms. The national parliament was now elected by direct vote, and the prime minister elected by the parliament. But it was quickly apparent after the first election in May 1981 that little had changed. Real power stayed in the palace. Nepal became a small but persistent part of Amnesty International reports.

The large amounts of foreign aid did little to help the average Nepali, who actually saw their economic situation deteriorate as Kathmandu's elite prospered.

The Last Straws

When the Trade Treaty between India and Nepal lapsed in March 1989, India severely restricted economic movement across the border, and Nepal's weak economy was crippled. Hardest hit were the urban areas that relied on kerosene to cook and on Indian imports for many staples.

In the spring of 1990, protests over shortages of basic foods evolved into demonstrations against corruption, lack of rights, and the ban on political parties. Dozens of semi-underground parties led by the underground NCP and several communist groups held demonstrations that immediately gained widespread support.

These parties, still illegal, formed an alliance to press their demands for democracy. By March 1990, even Nepal's civil servants took to the streets and the government was in serious trouble. Finally the king was forced to agree to demands for democracy.

After suffering for years in prison, Krishna Bhattrai was named prime minister (arriving at the official residence with a single

A Tamang woman, her baby on her back, votes in a local election. The vote is a very new thing after centuries of autocratic rule and still not well understood by everybody.

suitcase) and a coalition cabinet of Congress and communist members was named.

The palace dragged its heels on every question. Monarchy-supporting *goondas* (thugs) roamed at night. Statements from the palace confused whether the king had actually agreed to give up power or not.

Thousands of demonstrators marched through Kathmandu again in September to prevent the palace from backing out of its agreements.

The deadline for a new constitution passed. The palace made excuses to delay considering the draft constitution, then made a counter draft.

It was as if nothing had changed since the 19th century rumors and intrigues. Finally the alliance's draft was accepted by all parties, with Nepal's first multi-party elections in more than two decades taking place in early May 1991.

Chapter Two

THE NEPALI PEOPLE

Just as Nepal's physical geography is a study of the meeting of two land masses, its human geography is a study of the meeting of two very distinct bodies of people. From the south came Indo-Aryans (Caucasoid) and from across the Himalayas came Orientals (Mongoloid).

Nepal's 19 million people are distinguished not only by race, but by completely different religions, over a dozen languages, and a dozen distinct cultures. More than 50% of the population live below the poverty line.

Nepal is a nation of immigrants. People who crossed the high Himalayan passes stayed at the higher elevations, living near the top of ridges and in high valleys. People from the south settled in the low lying basins and river valleys that reminded them of the hot plains of India they had left behind.

Forced from their own homelands, victims of aggression themselves, they worked things out with their new neighbors peacefully. Tolerance, not confrontation, has marked their relations through the centuries.

Tolerance, but not assimilation. Each cultural group (and there are dozens) has maintained its own traditions. There has been little overt pressure on one group to adopt the religion or culture of another. Groups remain exclusive rather than inclusive. There has been little intermixing or intermarriage and most groups have social taboos to prevent such mixing, the strongest ones existing among caste Hindus.

THE CASTE SYSTEM IN NEPAL

Until the abolition of the caste system in 1963 there were institutionalized prohibitions as well. These prohibitions were ingrained in the society long before they were made laws, and eliminating the legislation has done little to change social attitudes. Intermarriage within Nepal's different groups remains rare.

Hindus are born into a particular position in the social hierarchy and in that position they remain for the rest of this life. Birth determines occupation (or range of occupations): people are born priest, merchant, or blacksmith. They do not have the option of changing their occupation; a blacksmith could not open a store and expect anyone other than members of his caste or lower to come. A Chhetri could not assume the responsibilities of a priest. Society ostracizes anyone who attempts to break these rules.

The Nepali caste system also stipulated where each caste can live, what they can wear, how they should address those above them, and what forms their ceremonies (births, weddings, and deaths) can take.

Your Name Is Your Job

Your name is your identity card, it tells your job, your position in society, who you can marry, and who you can associate with. Someone named Dhakal is a Brahmin, Karki is a Chhetri, Giri is Sunyeshi, Kami is a smith, Gwala keeps cattle, and Hajam is a barber. In the Terai, Halkhors clean the village latrines, Doms and Dushads dispose of carcasses and provide wood for funeral pyres.

However, there are exceptions to this rule. Mr Bhatta, for example, can be a Kumain Brahmin, a Purbiya Brahmin, or a Newar Brahmin. Mr Bista can be a Kumain Brahmin or a Chhetri.

To escape your caste you must change your name and move to a community where no one knows you and no one who knows you will ever come. This is not an easy thing to do. Furthermore you must stop all contact with your family.

The Code of Manu

The principles which govern the caste system grew out of the *Manusmriti*, the Laws of Manu. Manu is the mythical progenitor of mankind, the Hindu equivalent of Adam. The code he set out was first recorded some time after the *Vedas*, the Hindu scriptures, were recorded. So sacred was the *Manusmriti* that only Brahmins, the priestly caste, were allowed to read it.

The code divides society into four groups. Brahma is believed to have created mankind from his own body. The caste system ranks people according to the part of Brahma's body they were originally created from.

Brahmins, the priests and interpreters of the laws, placed themselves (not surprisingly) at the top of the caste hierarchy. They sprang from Brahma's head and mouth.

Ranking below the Brahmins are the Chhetris, who emerged from Brahma's arms and chest. The Brahmins are the keepers and interpreters of Hinduism, the Chhetris are its enforcers and defenders. They are the caste of warriors and rulers, the holders of secular

31

power. The King of Nepal comes from the Thakuri sub-caste of Chhetris.

Below these two groups come the Vaisyas, the traders, farmers, and craftsmen, who sprang from Brahma's thighs. They are the middle class of society.

At the bottom of the caste hierarchy are the Sudras, the so-called 'occupational castes', who are said to come from Brahma's feet. Feet are in contact with the earth, the source of all pollution. Sudras, arising from this pollution, are themselves polluted. Contact with them can spread their pollution. To prevent this, Hinduism placed severe restrictions on their rights to associate with the upper castes. Tailors, cobblers, and smiths are Sudras.

A group of Newar women of the sweeper caste move through Patan on their way to a job. Although the caste system no longer exists in law, many of the people still perform their traditional jobs and face old prejudices.

Rigid, But

Hinduism can also be flexible when its own survival is at stake. In the 12th century, when waves of Brahmins made their way across the jungles of the Terai of western Nepal, they found strong, long established kingdoms of people known as the Khas already there.

The Khas were Aryan and spoke a Sanskrit-based language, but had developed from a different branch from the Hindus of the plains. They drank liquor, had no dietary restrictions and practiced their own religion.

They should have been considered Sudra, and they would have to be treated as 'untouchables'.

That could have put the new immigrants in a very difficult position. The newly-arrived Brahmins got around this touchy situation by offering the Khas the option to convert to Hinduism as Chhetris. Many of them did, and were given all the rights and privileges of Chhetris.

Children born of Brahmin-Khas marriages were placed in a newly created ranking, Khatri Chhetri, usually referred to in modern Nepal as K.C.

Those Khas who did not convert are often referred to as 'Matwali Chhetri' (drinking Chhetri) and are not entitled to wear the sacred thread. There are still large communities of them in the far west (Jumla, Humla, and Mugu).

HINDU CASTE GROUPS

Half of all the Brahmins and Chhetris in Nepal live in the far western hills, where they form about 80% of the population. The remainder are spread over the rest of the country. In general they are farmers, just as their ancestors were in India.

Caste Hindus have Caucasian features, but dark complexions. Nepali is their mother tongue, an Indo-Aryan language brought with them when they migrated from India.

Except in the far west, Hindu caste groups tend to live at the lower elevations, below 1,800 m (6,000 ft) and often below 900 m (3,000 ft). After coming from the low-lying, rice-growing plains of northern India, they settled in the lower regions of the Middle Hills.

Settlements of Brahmins and Chhetris tend to be diffuse, scattered over a large area. A field and *khets* (irrigated rice terraces) often separate one home or family group from another. Each home will have a small altar outside, usually with a *tulsi* (basil) plant filling it.

Brahmins and Chhetris are still very dominant groups in hill society in Nepal. Even in areas where they are in minority, they tend to dominate by their superior economic position, their superior education, and their superior knowledge of the way things 'work' – bureaucratic regulations and laws, available government programs, local politics.

Brahmins

At the top of the Hindu caste system are the Brahmins, the priestly caste. They are forbidden by traditional caste laws from drinking alcohol and eating certain foods – onions, tomatoes, and eggs, for example.

The traditional role of Brahmins in society is to satisfy the community's spiritual needs. Only Brahmins are allowed to read and interpret the *Vedas* and other Hindu scriptures. Only Brahmins can conduct the elaborate *pujas* (worship services) necessary for special occasions.

Jaishis, a subgroup of Brahmins, are the descendants of illegitimate Brahmins. While they are considered Brahmins, they are not allowed to conduct religious services.

Special occasions that require Brahmins include *nwaran* (name-giving), *pasni* (rice-feeding, weaning), marriages, *kriya* (funeral services), and *shraddha* (annual ceremony for a dead person).

Brahmins are paid for their services, usually in cash and food. Offerings made during the service are retained by the officiating priest. During funeral services, for example, everything the dead person will need in their next life, including furniture and cooking utensils, are presented to the Brahmin conducting the rites.

A traditional way to gain religious merit is to present a Brahmin with a cow, which may be given as a form of payment for conducting a puja.

Brahmin Subdivisions

There are two major divisions: Purbiya (eastern) and Kumain (western). Kumain comes from Kumaon, the Indian district to the west of Nepal. Purbiya comes from *purba* (east). Both of these groups think they are of higher status than the other. It is often possible to determine which of these two subgroups a person belongs to simply by hearing their name. Bista, Khatiwada, Paitola, Pant, and Upreti are examples of Kumain names. Chapagain, Devkota, Khanal, Pokhrel, and Regmi are some of the names associated with Purbiya Brahmins.

Occupations

Being a priest is not a full-time job for most Brahmins and in fact many Brahmins do not perform priestly duties at all. To support themselves they usually have another profession.

Traditionally Brahmins (and Chhetris) were the only group that could read and write and had any education. This naturally led them to take up professions in which they could use those skills. Brahmins often became teachers and worked as civil servants. They are still prominent in both these professions. In addition they are often farmers, shopkeepers, and inn keepers.

Marriage

Brahmins are a very conservative group. They marry exclusively within their own caste. Parents arrange the marriage: even within the caste a marriage partner must be chosen from within a limited number of subgroups. A Brahmin's spouse will often come from outside the home area (see *The Nepali Life Cycle*).

Brahmins and Chhetris used to practice child marriage until recently. Child marriage is outlawed now, but is still practiced in rural Nepal.

Divorce

Divorce is almost non-existent. Brahmins and Chhetris believe marriage is not a matter of choice or accident. Marriage is predestined and continuous: we were married to the same person in our former life, we will be married to them again in the next. To divorce is a grave sin, breaking the sacred trust between man and God.

Polygamy

Polygamy is outlawed, but still exists and is openly tolerated in the hill areas. The most common justification given for polygamy is the inability of the wife to produce a son. Rich landowners may marry several times as a demonstration of their wealth.

Death

Both Brahmins and Chhetris cremate their dead by the side of a river soon after death. After the cremation, the ashes are thrown in the river. The lighting of the funeral pyre and conducting of the kriya (funeral rites) are perhaps the most important duties of a son. They ensure the peaceful passage of the dead soul to the next life. The rites can be performed by another male relative as a last resort, but only a son can guarantee swift and peaceful passage through death.

All Hindus wish to die and be cremated by the side of the Ganges, the holy river. If possible, Nepali Hindus will travel to Varanasi on the banks of the Ganges to die. Sometimes *asthi*, a small piece of bone from the cremation, will be saved to be taken to the Ganges later.

In Nepal, Pashupatinath on the outskirts of Kathmandu is the most holy place. The royal *ghats* (platforms for cremations) are there on the banks of the Bagmati River, at the foot of the stairs leading to the main temple. In the hills, *dobhans* (places where two rivers join) are considered especially holy and are often the site of local cremations.

Mourners are prohibited from eating meat, salt, lentils, oil, and a number of other foods during this time. The men shave their heads and do not receive a *tika* (a little bit of ash smeared on the forehead as a sign of blessing).

The men are also considered ritually polluted. They are forbidden from going to a temple or worshiping any deity. They are also forbidden from serving food or drink (including water) to any guests.

The eldest son of the dead person must observe an even stricter fast, eating only one meal a day consisting of rice, *ghyu* (clarified butter), and sugar. He must shave all the hair from his body and wear only a white scarf on his head and a white loin cloth. Each day he must conduct several hours of rituals supervised by a Brahmin involving ritual bathing with cold water several times. At the end of the mourning period, a big feast is held for the family and all those who attended the cremation.

The son will observe mourning for one year. Each year the dead person must be honored in a ceremony called 'shraddha', followed by a small feast in which a plate of food is offered to the dead soul.

Children: Saviors and Obligations

It is vital that a son be present to do these last funeral rites. If there is no son, the dead person's immortal soul could be in jeopardy.

Only a son can speed his parents on to heaven or on to a beneficial rebirth. The son also guarantees the family line will be carried on, another sacred obligation of the parents. Given the importance of a son, both in this life and the next, to the family line and to the parents' immortal souls, it is no wonder every man and woman desires at least one son.

Female children do not benefit their parents' souls; they only place a heavy sacred obligation on them. Finding a husband for their daughter is one of the greatest duties a couple has. If they are successful, they earn much merit, and if they fail, they lose much merit. If they are unable to keep their daughter pure until the time of the wedding, they also lose much merit.

Marrying the daughter can cost an enormous amount of money. The family may be forced to go into debt or sell some land to pay for the wedding. Once the daughter is married, she is no longer a member of her parents' household and the family can no longer count on her labor either.

The Janai: Symbol and Status

The *janai* (sacred thread) is a symbol of high status in the caste system. Only Brahmin and Chhetri men are allowed to wear this loop of three cotton threads above one shoulder, across the chest, and under the other arm. It signifies that the wearer is 'twice born'. His birth by his mother is his first, his initiation into Hinduism his second. When he is initiated into Hinduism, he receives the janai.

This initiation ceremony is called *bratabandha*. It combines a coming-of-age ceremony and a formal initiation into Hinduism. The janai's three intertwined threads symbolize the mind, the body, and the act of speech. The knots tied in the three threads as the janai is given symbolize the wearer's mastery of all three.

The janai must be kept literally and ritually clean. If it becomes frayed, dirty, or polluted (through contact with a woman during her menstruation, for example), it must be replaced. Men will sometimes drape it over their ear to prevent contamination while they go to the toilet or while bathing afterward.

The janai is replaced once a year on the day of the full moon of August, called Janai Purnima. On the day before, the wearer must completely clean himself: bathe, shave, cut his hair, his fingernails and toenails. He will eat only one meal, which must not contain any prohibited foods such as onion or garlic. He will eat no meat.

The ceremony may be performed at home by the family priest, or the wearer may go to a temple where several priests are waiting. The priest reads scriptures and then, invoking Vishnu, drapes the new, sanctified thread around the wearer's neck. The priest is then compensated for his service with money and food commensurate with the wearer's wealth and status.

Chhetris

Chhetris have much the same customs as Brahmins. In traditional society they were the warriors, the temporal authority to the priests' spiritual authority. The men of the Chhetri caste wear the janai just as Brahmin men do. They were considered the aristocracy of traditional society.

Chhetris have been sitting on the throne of Nepal for over 15 centuries, starting with the Licchavis who ruled Kathmandu from about the 4th century and who are believed to have been Rajputs.

The Shahs (the ruling family) are members of the Thakuri subgroup. Thakuris are the highest-ranking of the many Chhetri subgroups. The Ranas, who ruled as all-powerful hereditary prime ministers, are also Chhetri, but not Thakuri.

Chhetris settled in the same areas as the Brahmins. The Khas who didn't adopt Hinduism refer to themselves as Chhetri, and are referred to by others as Matwali (drinking) Chhetri. They cannot wear the janai.

In the Kharnali zone of far northwestern Nepal (including Humla and Jumla), large numbers of Chhetris live at high altitudes. They have adopted the same lifestyle as their Tibetan neighbors, growing the same crops and spending long periods of time on the road traveling to Tibet and back to Nepal as traders. This is the only area of the country with large numbers of Hindus living at high altitudes.

Occupations

The majority of Chhetris are subsistence farmers. As you'd expect, the military is a traditional occupation of Chhetris and even today many of Nepal's army officers are Chhetri. Large numbers of Chhetris continue to join the military, in Nepal, and the Gurkha contingents of the Indian and British armies.

Besides being warriors, they have traditionally held jobs that required the ability to read and write and have long been important in the government bureaucracy. They hold the same types of jobs the Brahmins do, except for being priests.

Social Customs

In their social customs and social relations, the Chhetris are close to the Brahmins. The men wear the janai. They are conservative, arrange their marriages, and rarely divorce.

They have some of the dietary restrictions of Brahmins. They are prohibited from drinking liquor, and have restrictions on who they will receive water and rice from.

The Occupational Castes

The Sudras (occupational castes) form an important segment of Nepal's hill population even though they receive little recognition. In spite of the vital services they perform for the communities they live in, they are subject to discrimination and prejudice by upper caste Hindus and the hill tribes.

In hill society the main groups of occupational castes are tailors (Damais), smiths (Kamis), and cobblers/leatherworkers (Sarkis).

Damais are the village musicians as well as the tailors, and are an indispensable part of any wedding or village celebration.

The Sudras' position at the bottom of the social ladder has left them at the bottom of the economic ladder, too. Few of them have been able to get any education, because of the stigma attached to associating with them in any way.

In a Tamang village, a Kami carves a wooden mask in the cattle stall below the house. As a member of the occupational caste, he is not allowed on the porch above where guests sit and family members work.

Even when talking to them, the low form of you, *timi*, will be used and often the even lower form, *ta* (used with animals), will be used.

Restrictions

Sudras would never be allowed in any of the other homes in the village. If they were required to enter a home to do some special work, the house owner would conduct a purifying puja after they have left. Some households will not even allow them on the outer porch.

Brahmin priests will not officiate at any of the religious rites of Sudras. Weddings, funerals and other ceremonies are conducted by a male relative of the family.

In rural areas, a member of this group would probably not enter a public tea shop and would hesitate to enter a shop of any kind. After eating or drinking at a tea shop, they are required to wash their own glasses and plates and leave them to dry; afterward the shop-keeper will wash them once more.

Even though the hill tribes are largely non-Hindu and are outside the caste system, they treat the occupational castes in almost exactly the same way as upper caste Hindus do. The hill tribes may be slightly more lenient toward Sudras, but in general they treat them as inferior, just as upper caste Brahmins do.

Economics and Changes

The occupational castes are generally landless with neither the money nor opportunity to buy any land. Ready-made clothes, shoes, tools, and other goods are becoming increasingly available in Nepal's hills. As this happens, they find that their traditional trades are needed less and less.

Restricted by the caste system as to the jobs open to them, the Sudras' economic position is becoming tougher and tougher. They are being forced to leave their traditional jobs that at least required a skill, and work as menial workers: porters, day laborers, and tenant farmers.

UPS AND DOWNS

Hinduism is a very conservative system: it is impossible to change your station in life upward during this lifetime. You can only strive to earn merit by correct and moral acts in this life and thereby receive a better position in your next life. The Brahmins, who control the spiritual life, and the Chhetris, who control the temporal, are in the best positions, but also have the most to lose.

You can't be rewarded in this life, but you can be punished. If you break the laws of your caste in this life, you may lose your caste in this life and doom yourself to a lower birth in the next. For heinous crimes, a person may find himself reborn as an animal or insect.

Low caste people earned their status by their actions in a previous life. They have violated the precepts of Hinduism and, because of this, are impure, polluted. To associate with them, by touch or accepting water or food from them, is to pollute yourself. You would risk a lower birth in the next life.

Would You Like A Drink of Water?

Drinking water is the basic test of a person's status. Water can purify anything, but it becomes polluted if handled by a person of lower caste. This polluted water then pollutes anything it touches. Who will take water from whom is the fundamental test of caste and status between people in Nepal.

A Brahmin would never think of taking water from a person of the occupational castes. But he would probably accept it if served by a member of the hill tribes, who are considered 'clean' even though they are non-Hindu and outside the caste system.

If a person touches a water vessel with their mouth, the water vessel becomes *jutho* (ritually polluted). The water must be emptied out and the vessel rinsed with water to purify it before it can be filled and used again.

Rice

Because rice is usually cooked with water, special injunctions are observed on who will eat rice cooked by whom. Some Brahmins will only eat rice they prepare themselves; others only eat rice cooked by someone of equal or higher caste than themselves.

Rice is a sacred food itself, but the key seems to be the water it's cooked in. A Brahmin might eat rice cooked in milk, even if it was prepared by someone they would not normally accept rice cooked in water from.

Debt and Credit in Rural Nepal

Until quite recently there was no widespread banking system. Even now a bank may be days away and banking practices are strange and disconcerting to most farmers. The richer Brahmins often act as moneylenders for the entire community.

Credit, the ability to borrow money, is an important fact in the lives of Nepal's farmers. Most farmers work small holdings that often cannot even produce enough to provide for the household. Loans are often necessary simply to feed the family.

Casual short-term loans between neighbors are common and no interest is charged on these. For larger loans, the person wanting the loan must go to a rich local farmer.

Loans may be made in the form of cash or grain for food. The interest charged on these loans is generally between 10–15%. If the person is desperate for money, a higher interest may be charged. For short-term loans an interest of around 5% per month is charged.

There are many ways to repay the loan. Of course, the cash or grain may be repaid in kind, but the economics of the typical farmer often make this impossible. The debtor may exchange their labor in return for cancellation of some portion of their debt or at least their interest. Because the creditor determines how much the labor given is worth, the debtor can find they have made no progress toward repaying ther principal and may even be losing ground on their interest. The debtor becomes a *de facto* indentured servant.

The other chief creditor in any village is the local storekeeper, who may also be a Brahmin. Villagers in cash-poor Nepal often require a loan to make their purchases. Almost every rural shopkeeper has a register or a simple notebook full of debts and repayments for each household in the village.

If the debt is repaid within six months, little or no interest is charged. For older debts, an interest of 15% or more is charged.

THE HILL TRIBES AND THE CASTE SYSTEM

The hill tribes are outside the caste system, but in general they are considered somewhere in the middle: without the high status of Brahmins and Chhetris, but also without the severe restrictions of the occupational castes.

Many of the tribes are increasingly influenced by Hinduism and will call in Brahmin priests to conduct important ceremonies connected with births, deaths, and marriages.

Most of the hill tribes practice the same prohibitions on the occupational castes as their Hindu neighbors. They will not allow a Kami (blacksmith), for example, into their home or even on their porch. They may not even allow him to cook in their yard. A person of the hill tribes would not accept water or rice from a blacksmith anymore than a high-caste Hindu would.

With the hill tribes, though, these restrictions are much more a matter of the individual household's feelings, not mandated by the tribe's social code.

Origins and Life

A number of Tibeto-Burmese tribes crossed the Himalayas to settle in Nepal. Each tribe has remained separate: proud and culturally self-sufficient. All these tribes have Oriental features as opposed to the Aryan-featured Hindus. The tribes were Buddhist originally, but some are coming under increasing Hindu influence.

The hill tribes live as high as 3,000 m (9,900 ft). This is too high to grow much rice. Millet, corn, wheat, and potatoes are their main crops. The grains are roasted, ground into flour, and boiled with water into a thick paste called *dhedo*. Dhedo is the staple food of the Middle Hills. Sometimes pancake-like unleavened bread, *roti*, is made, cooked on a dry skillet.

Most families, if they can afford it, keep herds of goats and live-stock. A large herd of goats is a sign of wealth. The wool of the goats traditionally supplied the clothes for the tribes. Sheep are still an important source of wool, meat, and cash (from sales). In the monsoon the livestock is taken to high, isolated pastures at altitudes exceeding 4,000 m in some places.

These high pastures are called *ghots* (similar to a stable). Usu-ally only one or two family members go, the rest stay home to work the farm. Rich families hire someone to take the animals for them. Ghots and the time spent at them are an important part of the culture, particularly for adolescents.

Many of the hill tribes' men carry a *khukuri*, the traditional curved-blade knife of Nepal, handily tucked in their long waist sash.

Hill tribe villages are usually compact clusters of houses. Adja-cent houses may even share a wall. The streets of the village are often paved with stone. Individual homes may have a courtyard paved with stone in front of the house.

Hill tribe society is very liberal compared to that of the Hindu castes. They often work as day laborers and porters, just as the occupational castes do.

Women

Hill tribes are patriarchal, like the caste groups, but women have more freedom than they do in Hindu caste society. Women feel

A man carries a pile of fodder for his livestock. Nepal's landscape and poverty make machines of any kind a rare sight. Everything depends on the strong backs and hands of the people.

more confident to express their opinion in private and even some-times in public. Far from hiding their faces, young women of the hill tribes speak freely and even flirt good naturedly. Older members of the tribe see nothing wrong with this (they often enjoy the flirting just as much).

It is not unusual for a mixed group of men and women to take a portering job together, traveling and living together for weeks. It's very hard to think of caste Hindu women doing this, or of Hindu men allowing their women to do this.

No great stigma is attached to a woman who bears a child out of wedlock, or to the child either. Divorce is not common, but does occur. The divorced woman may marry again. Widows too may marry again, and there is no stigma to a young man marrying an older woman, even if she is very much older.

Marriage

Inter-tribal marriage is still very rare, but within their own tribe young people are often free to find their own spouse. Richer fami-lies may arrange the marriages of their children, but do not feel the same sense of religious obligation as Hindus. Some tribes favor a cross-cousin marriage and almost all tribes recognize kidnaping or capture as a legitimate way for a man to find his bride (see *The Nepali Life Cycle*).

Divorce

Divorce is frowned on, but even though there is no special divorce mechanism, most hill tribes do recognize it may occur and have a way to deal with it. A marriage may be dissolved by mutual consent. If a man takes another's wife (this may involve physically kidnap-ing the woman), he must pay the woman's husband a compensation. The amount of the compensation may be worked out by the parties involved or based on the judgment of the village elders.

Clan Hierarchy

Just as the Hindus have the caste system, each tribal group has its own hierarchy of clans. These family groups are called *jaats* or *thars*. In some hill groups these jaats and thars may be even subdivided into smaller family groups.

Some tribes give higher status to some clans within the tribe. Gurungs, for example, are divided into two groups: *char-jaat* (four jaat) and *sora-jaat* (16 jaat). The two groups do not intermarry and the char-jaat are considered to be of higher status than the sora-jaat.

While questions of jaat may arise when a wedding is involved, divisions of jaats and thars in hill tribe society are not the powerful force that caste is within Hindu society. The degree of importance and status attached to the different jaats and thars varies from tribe to tribe, but in general tribe members view each other as equals.

When tribe members from different villages meet, they may inquire what the other's jaat is or they may not. Even if they do ask, there is not the same importance and establishment of status that happens among Hindus. Most tribes use their tribal name, not their clan name. Magars sometimes use their thar name either alone or with Magar, e.g.: Thapa or Thapa Magar, Rana or Rana Magar.

Occupations

By and large the hill tribes remain tied to their steep hillsides. The overwhelming majority are subsistence farmers. Poor education has limited the access of the hill tribes to jobs in government and commerce.

During the dry winter months the men may venture to towns in the Terai or even as far as India looking for day labor work that will give the cash to make ends meet.

The hill tribes, men and women alike, work as porters throughout the hills of Nepal and as unskilled laborers wherever they can find work.

The Military

The other main employment of the hill tribes is the military, particularly in the Indian and British armies where they are world-famous as the Gurkha soldiers.

The military is an honored profession for young men, and the periodic recruitment camps are extremely competitive. The money sent back by these soldiers and their pensions after they retire are the main source of cash in the Middle Hills. Their income is an important part of Nepal's national economy as well.

It is not an easy job. The soldiers are gone from their villages for years at a time. During the brief visits home a wife must be found, a family started. Soldiers are only allowed to bring their family with them for one three-year term during their entire time in the military. A soldier may retire hardly knowing his own family.

But he retires with a pension and (usually) a firm financial footing, and there is still no shortage of recruits.

Former soldiers are often a source of new ideas and innovations when they return to their village. In Nepal returning soldiers were among the first to form an opposition group against the Ranas.

The changing status of Hong Kong in particular has made the future of the Gurkhas in the British army uncertain. There have been cutbacks in the recent past and more cutbacks seem inevitable. This may be a 'filler' in the world news, but it is vitally important to the hills of Nepal. The Gurkhas remain a source of pride and hope for Nepal and the tribes of the Middle Hills.

Religion

Most of the hill tribes would describe themselves as Buddhist. But there is usually a strong strain of animism and their own local religion mixed in, with Hinduism becoming more influential.

Magars, who tend to live farther south than the other tribes, have had more contact with Hindus and often say they are Hindu. They call Brahmin priests to conduct Hindu rites at their important events.

Gurungs sometimes do this as well, but Tamangs and the tribes in the east maintain their old beliefs.

Mixed in with Buddhism there is usually continuing respect and observance of older animist traditions too. A house may have its own household god to placate and call on a *jankri* (shaman) to cure sickness or cleanse a home of evil spirits.

TRIBAL GROUPS

In eastern Nepal the predominant groups are Rais and Limbus. These two tribes have a very long history in Nepal. With the Newars of the Kathmandu Valley, they probably have been in Nepal longer than any other group.

Rais and Limbus

Rais and Limbus are descended from the Kiratis. They were pushed out of the valley and retreated east, the direction they had come from originally. Even today Rais and Limbus are known as Kiratis or Kirantis.

They inhabit the eastern districts of Nepal including Taplejung, Panchtar, Illam, Terhathum, Sankhuwasabha, Bhojpur, Khotang, and Solukhumbu.

Many of the men carry large khukuris tucked in their belts, and always have a *topi* (a small flat hat, the national headwear of Nepal) tipped jauntily on their head. Limbus in particular have a reputation for being quick tempered and ready to use their khukuris at the drop of a topi.

Both groups are famed for their service as Gurkha soldiers. They also work in the tea plantations of Illam and Darjeeling and travel all over India for work.

A term of respect for Limbus is 'Subba'. Sometimes this is used as a last name. Rais and Limbus have their own religious leaders, *nokchhoes* and *fedangmas*. Both types of priest are in touch with the local gods of their tribe and are a type of shaman.

A typical Limbu teenager dressed in traditional clothing.

Each group has its own calendar of rites and rituals to be conducted throughout the year. They also observe Hindu religious festivals such as Dasain and Tihar.

Limbus and some Rais bury their dead in a community ground that resembles a Western cemetery. Rais often build multi-tiered monuments over the body. Some Rais bury their dead in a field near their home.

Tamangs

Tamangs are one of the largest tribal groups in Nepal. They mainly live in the hills north of Kathmandu, but there are also small groups in the east and the far west. The name Tamang is derived from the Tibetan word for 'horse trader', which gives an idea of their origins and their former profession.

Tamangs are Buddhist with their own lamas, who may go to Tibet to study. Major villages have a *gompa* (Buddhist monastery or worship center). Some Tamang lamas are skillful painters of Buddhist *thangka* paintings, a style normally associated with Tibetans.

A Tamang village may be marked by a Tibetan-style *chorten* at the entrance and *mane* walls (constructed of stones carved with Buddhist scripture and drawings).

Tamangs also use *jankris*, shaman faith healers who expel the illness through chants and blowing on the affected part of the body. The jankris are also consulted to worship local and clan deities.

Tamangs cremate their dead on a hilltop. A lama conducts the ceremony and everyone attending brings wood for the cremation.

Tamang communities are well known for their independence and their resistance to and suspicion of outside authority. They have suffered economically as a result. Until recently there were few functioning schools in their communities and they seldom receive government services or development aid.

Others have used the Tamangs' lack of education and lack of knowledge to exploit them. Tamang men are a familiar sight in

Kathmandu working as porters, pushing the carts called *tela gardhis* through the streets, or waiting for their next job in short sleeve woolen jackets made by their household's women.

Gurungs

Gurungs, linguistic cousins of the Tamangs, live mainly in the hills of Lamjung and Kaski above Pokhara. They have substantial villages; Gandruk, the largest, has over 700 homes.

The Gurungs have a long history in Nepal. Their military tradition has continued to the present day. They are one of the largest sources of Gurkha soldiers and it's a rare house that doesn't have a strong military connection.

The money sent home by soldiers and the pensions of ex-Gurkhas have given some Gurung villages a prosperity rare in the hills of Nepal.

Like all hill tribes their villages tend to be near the top of the ridge, with most of their fields below the village in a cascade of terraces, sometimes going all the way down to the river. It can take an hour or more to descend to the warmer riverside khets where families cultivate their small amounts of rice.

Gurungs are herders as well as farmers, with large herds of goats and sheep. Rich Gurungs hire someone to take their herds to the high pastures during the monsoon, but most people must send a member or two of the family.

Gurungs at one time were Buddhist with their own lamas, but increasingly they are turning to Brahmins to conduct their religious services. They also turn to jankris in times of illness.

Gurungs may bury or cremate their dead, but with the increasing influence of Hinduism, this may be changing.

The Rodi

As Gurung children reach adolescence, groups of boys (or girls) band together to form a club of 10–15 members called a *rodi*, a kind of teenage support group. The rodi needs an adult to be their chaperone (for the boys a man, the girls a woman) and provide them with a space to use as a combination clubhouse and dormitory.

During the day the rodi functions as a labor cooperative. The members take turns working in each other's fields, collecting firewood, and helping to graze each other's livestock.

At night they gather again in the clubhouse and sing, dance, talk, and ponder all the questions teenagers can think of. As the rodi's members get older, a boy rodi will establish a relationship with a girl rodi in the village. At night the boys will go to the girls' clubhouse to visit and exchange songs and dances, returning to their own clubhouse late at night.

As the club gets even older, they will plan day and overnight trips to other villages and to local fairs and festivals. Girls' clubs from other villages invite boys' rodis to visit. The girls will prepare special food, and songs and dances. The boys' visit might last several days. If the members are old enough, romance and marriages can develop.

The rodi disbands when the members reach 18 and start to marry. The rodi provides a unique and valuable way for teenagers to make that difficult transition from child to adult. But it is fading out rapidly, another victim of the rapid changes in Gurung culture.

Magars

Magars live in central and western Nepal too, but generally farther west, or south, and at lower (and warmer) elevations. Magars are one of the largest of the hill tribes, with settlements in Tanahu, Kaski, Syangje and as far west as Rukum, Rolpa, and Sallyan.

They were one of the earliest tribes to migrate into Nepal. Their main area in western Nepal was so thickly populated it used to be referred to as the Bara Magaranth (12 Magar areas).

Because they are the southernmost of the hill tribes, they have had the longest and heaviest contact with caste Hindus migrating north from India. Not surprisingly the Magars are the most heavily Hindu-influenced of the hill tribes, often calling Brahmin priests to hold their religious services.

The Magar language is disappearing slowly and many Magars grow up speaking Nepali in their home as their first language.

Magars are farmers but, living at lower altitudes away from the high pastures, are not the great herders Gurungs are. The other major income source is the military. The Magars have the largest representation of all of Nepal's groups in the military. They were rated the best soldiers when the British started recruiting in the 19th century and were consequently given preference during recruiting.

Magars were also traditionally highly regarded as craftsmen (masons, carpenters, builders, miners) and often worked in Nepal's now-defunct mines.

The Thakalis

Far up the valley of the Kali Gandaki lives a small group of people called Thakali, whose fame and reputation are much larger than their numbers. The group takes its name from *Thak Khola* (river), the name given to the Kali Gandaki from Ghasa to Jomsom. Their 'capital' is the town of Tukche, which was once prosperous from salt trade monopoly and seeing new prosperity from recent tourism.

A terrible wind throws rocks down this dry, high valley everyday. It's a very inhospitable, capricious place to live in, and Thakalis learned long ago it couldn't be depended on to provide a living.

Occupations

Building on a contract from the Nepali government granting them a monopoly on the lucrative salt trade with Tibet, the Thakalis have developed into one of the most successful long-distance trading and the most astute business groups in Nepal.

As Thakalis spread outside their small valley setting up business and trade throughout central Nepal, they set up hotels too.

Today Thakali hotels (famous for their hospitality and excellent cuisine) dot the towns and cities of central Nepal and are the standard by which all Nepali hotels are judged. Thakali *dal-bhaat-tarkaari* (lentils, rice, and curried vegetables) is the choice of any Nepali on the road.

Private Financing

The Thakalis are a very tightknit community. To help develop businesses without going outside their community, they have developed a system called *dhigur*.

About 25 people come together to form a group. Each year the members of the group put a set amount of money in a pool. Each year a different member of the dhigur gets to take that money and use it as they wish. The member is chosen by lottery, by bidding, or sometimes based on immediate need. A person may belong to several dhigurs at a time or organize a new one if they want to start a business and need money.

Religion and Clans

The Thakalis are composed of four clans, each with its own clan god: Gauchan (dragon), Tulachan (elephant), Sherchan (lion), and Bhattachan (yak). Their religion is a mixture of all the religions that have passed up and down their narrow valley: Buddhism, Hinduism, Bon-po (the pre-Buddhist religion of Tibet), and Jankri-ism.

Buddhist gompas are found throughout their towns, but Buddhism is often looked down on these days as the religion of Bhotes and Tibetans, who in turn are looked down on as poor and backward. Hinduism is increasing in popularity, like in the rest of the Middle Hills. Jankri-ism is also a strong force in their communities.

BHOTES AND THE HIMALAYAN PEOPLES

All across the northern third of Nepal the Himalayan mountains rise up to double (and more) the heights of the Middle Hills. Tucked in the high (above 3,000 m or 9,872.5 ft), narrow valleys between these giants are settlements of Bhotiya, or Bhotes, collective terms for several distinct ethnic groups living here that compose 10% of Nepal's population.

If you ask, many of these people will say they are Gurung. There may be truth to this, but it is also due to the way most Nepalis look down on Bhotes.

Bhote is not a name which is worn with much pride these days. Bhote means 'bumpkin' to many Nepalis: their clothes are different (and often very dirty), their food is different, their Nepali is often mediocre, and their religion is not the same as that of the Hindu majority.

Their languages, cultures and religion are basically Tibetan. There are Tibetan Buddhist gompas everywhere. Buddhism is a central force in the lives of the people here.

A few villages practice an even older Shamanist religion called Bon-po. The Sherpa community has a series of dances called Mani Rimdu, performed in the spring and autumn, which celebrate the victory of Buddhism over Bon-po. There are no obvious differences between Bon-po and Buddhist villages, both may have gompas, chortens, and mane walls, but in the Bon-po communities, people keep to the right as they walk around them.

The amounts of potatoes, barley, and buckwheat that grow at these altitudes are insufficient to supply one year's food. People raise large herds of goats, sheep and yaks, and use them to carry goods for trade.

Many people dig a type of root cellar for winter food storage. People rely on meat for a larger portion of their diet, drying and storing it for long periods of time.

Although Buddhists eat meat, they have a prohibition against killing. Sometimes Hindus or hill tribes men are brought in to slaughter animals that the village then divides up. Animals sometimes meet with 'accidents', a fall off the trail, for example.

A Bhote loads his yaks with grain to trade in Tibet. His large bags are woven from yak hair.

Tea mixed with salt and butter is the staple drink. The taste is strange at first, but most people grow fond of it rapidly. The other diet staple here is *tsampa*, roasted buckwheat and barley flour mixed together. It is often simply mixed with tea into a paste or dough and eaten. It can also be made into a flat, unleavened, pancake-shaped bread.

Women

There are Buddhist nuns, but in very small numbers compared to monks. Bhote women are open and friendly, and when in groups working in the fields, sometimes heckle passing men with ribald taunts. The women generally have more rights and say in family and their own personal matters. In tourist areas it's not unusual for a woman to manage a hotel while her husband is away for months at a time.

Sherpas

The most well-known group of Bhotes are the Sherpas, who are centered in the Solokhumbu area. Many tourists now say 'Sherpa' for any guide or porter, but actually it should only be used for the tribe living in the high valleys of the Everest region in eastern Nepal.

Born at altitudes of more than 3,650 m (12,000 ft) at the base of the highest mountains in the world, Sherpas are naturally acclimated to high altitudes. They are justly renowned for their mountain climbing abilities, and their bravery and courage while climbing.

Sherpas settled in the Everest area about 300 years ago after crossing from Tibet. They were well known as traders long before their fame as mountain porters and guides. They are experts at crossbreeding yaks and cows, the result (the male is called *dzopkyo*, the female, *dzum*) being a better animal than either of the parents. They had a lucrative trade for these half-breeds in Tibet until the communists came.

The closing of the Tibetan border by the communist Chinese hurt them severely economically and it was only after the opening of Mt Everest to tourists that prosperity returned.

Manangis

Behind the Annapurna Massif lies the small valley of Manang. The people who live here are known collectively as Manangis. The enormous Annapurnas cut off most rain, turning this 3,000 m (9,900 ft) high valley into a semi-arid, semi-arctic waste. Potatoes, barley, and buckwheat are about all that grow and most families can't even grow enough to feed themselves. There's not enough fodder to support large herds of sheep or yaks, either. Long ago the Manangis turned to long-distance trade to make ends meet and, today, they are the most famous (and infamous) traders in Nepal.

Two centuries ago the king of Nepal recognized both their harsh environment and their business acumen. He granted the people of Nyesyang (the proper name for the Manang Valley above Pisang) special trading privileges. As a result Manangis could travel and trade much more easily and with less restrictions than their fellow citizens.

It is only human nature that some people tried to take advantage of the Manangis' special position and, as Nepal became more involved with the modern world, Manangis were lured into the lucrative smuggling trade between Nepal, India, and the rest of the world. Gold, drugs, and art have been added to their merchandise; America and Europe added to their destinations.

Some Manangis have become incredibly rich. Palatial Manangi homes dot Kathmandu, but some have also become well known to the Nepali police and Interpol. In Nepal, 'Manangi' has become almost synonymous with 'smuggling' and their reputation is far from good.

Back in their home valley, though, the majority of Manangis continue to struggle to make ends meet. Tourists have recently started to give their valley an economic boost, but it is still a hard place to live in, with few chances for education or health services.

Manangis consider themselves Gurungs; the Gurungs to the south say they aren't, but their languages are very similar. Taller and more robust than their southern neighbors, dressed Tibetan style, they look ready to take on any challenge that comes their way.

THE NEWARS AND THE CASTE SYSTEM

The Newars are a self-contained society mirroring Nepali society as a whole. They have a complete caste system of their own, including 64 occupational castes. The classifications for a caste occupation could be very precise:

Castes	Surnames	Traditional Occupations
Bhatta Brahmin	Bhatta	temple priests
Gubhaju	Vajracharya	family priests
Udas	Lohaka	masons
Udas	Madika	confectioners
Khusa	Khusa, Tandukar	palanquin bearers
Nau	Napit	barbers, nailcutters
Tepe	Chitrakar	painters (artists)
Kulu	Kulu	drum makers
Chami	Chami, Chamkhala	sweepers

The ranking and hierarchy of caste can go on and on. The Nau caste has the low caste job of nailcutting, a very important part of some ceremonies. But they would only perform this service for people of the Jyapu farming caste and higher; anyone else would have to ask an even lower caste butcher to perform this service.

Even Buddhist Newars, who form a large portion of the Newar population, observed this caste system, and developed a hereditary priestly class.

During the golden age of Nepal from about the 15th century to the 18th century, Newari craftsmen made the valley's masterpieces in stone, brick, wood, and metal. The creative vitality and inspiration of these anonymous artists, as great as any in the world, continue to give energy and spirit to life in the valley.

The Newars' origins are unclear, but they have certainly been in the valley longer than any other group, some even say since prehistoric times.

Only in the Newari people have the Tibeto-Burmese and Indo-Aryan waves of migration mixed. One of the results of this mix is the Newari language. Although rooted in Sanskrit, it has been heavily influenced by the Tibeto-Burmese languages, and the resulting composite is one of the most complex and difficult languages in the world.

There is also a Newari script, but it has largely been replaced by Devenagri.

One theory is that the name 'Nepal' itself was derived from 'Newar'. Certainly the Newars form their own 'nation'. Inside the valley they are a microcosm of Nepal, split between Hindus and Buddhists, with people of both Aryan and Tibeto-Burmese ancestry calling themselves Newari and sharing a common culture and language. It is like a parallel society living within the larger Nepali one.

Urban Society

Newari society is an urban one. People live in densely packed towns. Even the farmers live in town and walk out to their fields each morning. Houses may be three or four stories high. Newars usually share common walls with their neighbors. Buildings run right up to the street's curb.

Homes are often packed around a small courtyard entered from the main street by a low, inconspicuous door. Larger courtyards have a stupa or temple in the middle. Kitchens are on the top floor of the house, so that cooking fumes can escape. Most homes have a rooftop terrace the family uses extensively for drying foods and clothes, as a kitchen workspace, and for sitting outside to enjoy the winter sunshine.

Inside these houses are large, strong joint families, usually three generations. The oldest active male makes decisions for the household and controls its finances.

Women are by no means powerless and have a say in household decisions. When a son marries, the new wife is more easily accepted into the husband's household than in caste Hindu society. As Newari society is an urban one with more access to schools, more Newar girls get an education.

At the same time Newars are very conservative and still arrange most of their marriages.

A typical urban scene in the predominantly Newar town of Bhaktapur. Some of the houses show the rooftop terrace common to Newari homes.

Newari society contains both Hindus and Buddhists and many people actually are both.

There is a long Buddhist tradition. Patan is one of the oldest Buddhist settlements anywhere in the world and still has a large portion of Buddhists.

There are large numbers of Buddhist stupas and *bahas* (monasteries) throughout the cities of the valley, but many of them are deserted or almost deserted.

There is also a caste of Newari Brahmin priests. Marriage between people of the two faiths is extremely rare, despite the fact that a family may call in a Buddhist priest for some ceremonies and a Brahmin for others.

The Kumari

The two faiths come together in the Kumari, the 'living goddess' who lives in her own palace next to the old royal palace at Hanuman Dokha. This small girl is believed to be an incarnation of the Hindu goddess Kanya Kumari. Buddhist Tantric priests are responsible for finding the new incarnation when the old Kumari becomes a mortal by reaching puberty or bleeding from a wound.

There are actually a dozen or so kumaris living throughout the valley's Newar settlements. The one living at Hanuman Dokha is the royal Kumari, and therefore the most important one.

Generous Hosts

Newar cuisine goes far beyond the usual dal-bhaat-tarkaari and there are many distinctly Newari dishes. Liquor is an important part of most celebrations and Newari *raksi* can be particularly potent.

The test for a good raksi is to dip your finger in it, then hold a lit match to it. If your finger puffs into a blue flame, then the raksi is strong enough.

Newars celebrate name-giving, rice-feeding and bratabandha ceremonies. There are also celebrations to particular gods or to celebrate particular events. Newars are famous for being big spenders on celebrations. They will spend far more than it seems they possibly can to ensure that the guests have the best food and drink.

Most of the great festivals of the valley, particularly Indra Jatra, Raato Machhendranath, Bisket Jatra, and Gai Jatra, are by and large Newari festivals. Newars have their own calendar. New Year's Day falls during the Tihar celebrations and Year 1 was A.D. 880.

Rites

Most Newari groups cremate their dead by the side of the river. In most cases the deceased belonged to a cremation *guthi* (see below). The members of the guthi come to the house and assist in the funeral rites. When all are present, the body, wrapped in a colored shroud, is carried on a green bamboo bier to the river with a large crowd of mourners following. Thirteen days of mourning follow for the family. Mourning lasts a year for the son, with similar rites and prohibitions as for caste Hindus.

Guthis

A powerful force in Newari society are the various guthis (social organizations) a person belongs to. A guthi can be social, religious, or economic. Most adults belong to several.

Guthis are formed for everything from maintaining the neighborhood's public facilities to managing a temple to holding joint farmlands to funeral associations.

Most families belong to a religious guthi composed of the extended family. Service guthis are based on common neighbors with membership drawn from several different castes. Membership in these two types of guthis is usually compulsory and inherited.

There are other guthis that are purely social organizations. Membership in some of these guthis is a sign of high social standing and is treated as an honor.

Guthis function like a committee. They sometimes settle disputes between the members. Members can be expelled or fined for offenses based on the vote of the membership. Offenses can mean anything from poor attendance to failure to carry out work assigned by the guthi to behavior disrupting the community (for example, breaches of caste or ritual, cheating customers, cheating on your wife). The chairman is usually the oldest member of the guthi.

OUTSIDE THE VALLEY

There are several small ethnic groups, usually confined to a specific area or geographic zone. There may be only a few thousand in the group, but they have their own distinct language and culture and consider themselves (and are considered by their neighbors) an independent community. Most of these groups live in very economically depressed areas.

They are usually shy and reclusive. With little education or knowledge of the outside world, they are easily exploited by their neighbors. Their position is, if anything, becoming more precarious.

Chepangs

An example is the Chepang tribe. They are traditionally hunters and gatherers living in the southern Middle Hills of central Nepal where the districts of Dhading, Mukwanpur, Gurkha, and Chitwan come together.

Only in the last few generations have Chepangs started to farm and stop relying on what they could find in the forests, and live in more permanent settlements.

Their traditional territory is sandwiched between the Tamangs above them and the caste Hindus who live below them. The Chepangs are taken advantage of by both, going into debt, particularly to Brahmins, and sometimes losing their land.

The Nepali government has a special program to help the Chepangs in their transition from hunter/gatherer to an agricultural life, but there is still a long way to go before they can even approach the standard of their subsistence farmer neighbors.

After centuries of living apart in the forests, avoiding contact with their neighbors, Chepangs are still timid and reclusive. There are still few Chepang children in schools, and they still have little knowledge of the world, even the country, outside their steep hillside homes.

THE TERAI

The Terai will soon hold more than 50% of Nepal's population. It is by far the most productive area of Nepal. The people in the Terai are more recent settlers than the people of the hills and still feel more cultural and economic affinity for their ancestral home, India, than for their 'new' home.

The Nepali government has resettled thousands from the Middle Hills and encouraged thousands more to come down from the hills in an attempt to build a Nepali identity in the Terai. The profile of the Terai's population, once overwhelmingly caste Hindu, is changing rapidly with these migrations.

The Terai is the only area in Nepal with a sizable Moslem population. In some places, Nepalgunj in the west for example, Moslems are in majority.

The Terai and The Hills

The Terai border between India and Nepal is basically an open one, with people of the area moving freely across it. Without the geographic barriers the hills present, the people settling in the Terai

WHICH VALLEY ARE YOU FROM?

have maintained close ties with their neighbors to the south. Their language and culture are like those of their southern neighbors.

Even in areas where the Terai and the hills overlap, the people of the Terai have a stronger relationship with their Indian neighbors than their Nepali countrymen. They look to the south for their spouses, and their socio-economic relationships ignore the political border.

People in the hills smile at the *lungi*-clad *terai-wallas* hunkered and shivering in hill bazaars, a basket of tomatoes on sale at their feet. People in the Terai grin at the bandy-legged *pahardis* down from the hills, bewildered and dodging cars and rickshaws in the crowded bazaars.

Because of its proximity to India, where the caste system originated, divisions and prohibitions have always been more clearly enforced in the Terai than in the Middle Hills.

The Caste System in The Terai

Economic status is closely tied to caste in the Terai. The higher the caste, the higher the economic standing of the family.

Caste occupations are more specific. Every possible job seems to have its own caste. Lohars make iron farming implements, Badahis make wooden implements and carts. Mallahas are fishermen and row the ferries, Dhobis wash clothes, Telis press oil, and Halwalis make the sweets for weddings and feasts.

Until recently these job divisions were strictly enforced: the Halwalis' clothes were washed by the Dhobis.

Relationships among groups of neighbors would develop and continue across generations, often under the patronage of a local landowner who paid the occupational castes a retainer in addition to their fees. The size of the retainer and fee depends on the wealth of the landlord. There is competition and even buying and selling of the best landlords within the occupational caste community.

Villages

Settlements tend to be a tightknit cluster of wattle-and-daub, thatch-roofed one-story houses. Villages are grids of interlocking units of fenced houses and courtyards joined by narrow alleys. The village is situated in the middle of fields, an island in a lake of cultivation.

A rich landowner's house may dominate the village. It is of better quality, often concrete and brick with a large covered arcade. Television antennas are a common sight on these houses now.

Relationships

Social relations in the home tend to be very conservative. Women will often cover their face with a corner of their sari as if by a reflex action. A woman's world is largely confined to her home and village. Some rich, upper caste families even construct a separate unit for women to live and work in and to quarter the women and married men. A separate building is used for business and entertaining guests.

Changing Situation

The Terai is the fastest growing, fastest developing, and fastest changing area of Nepal outside the Kathmandu Valley.

At the same time as it is trying to stop the migration from the south (with limited success), the Nepali government has been encouraging migration from the Middle Hills. This policy grew from the opening up of large areas of the Terai, beginning in the 1950s by using DDT to eliminate the malaria-bearing mosquitoes that made it impossible to clear the jungles.

The availability of new land combined with a land reform and redistribution policy and overpopulation in the Middle Hills enabled large groups of people to relocate to the Terai. These new landowners include large numbers of hill tribe members as well as caste Hindus.

This is in the Nepali government's self interest. The Terai is vital to Nepal's survival, yet the people of the Terai have traditionally felt stronger ties to their cultural home: India. As people from the Middle Hills move down to the Terai, the area becomes more closely tied to the rest of the country.

The economic changes brought by the availability of mass produced food and goods is changing the job and social roles of the occupational castes in the Terai, just as it is in the hills. Undoubtedly the influx of people from the hills will also have some liberalizing effect on the caste system of the Terai.

Tharus

Although the Terai is dominated by caste Hindus today, for centuries the Tharus had it to themselves. They had developed a natural immunity to aul, the dreaded malaria that made a trip through the Terai like a game of Russian roulette.

The Tharus cleared small villages in the jungle surrounded by fields, ringed in by thick jungles full of tigers, elephants, rhinos, poisonous snakes, and the aul.

Today the jungle has by and large disappeared, and the new rich farmlands are dominated by the newly arrived Hindus and hill tribes migrating down from the Middle Hills.

The Tharus, spread all across the Terai and into India, are one of the largest ethnic groups in the country. But after living isolated in their jungle homes for centuries, they were ill-prepared for the rapid development of their home territory. Their new neighbors, with greater knowledge of laws and the modern world in general, have taken advantage of the Tharus time and again, and they remain one of Nepal's poorest groups.

Many of them have become tenant farmers on land they formerly owned, and many are deeply in debt to the rich landowners around them.

Tharus are Mongoloid, their language a mix of several North Indian languages. Their villages are tight clusters of houses with thatched or tiled roofs and mud and cow dung plaster walls. Sometimes they decorate their walls with animals in relief.

They are strongly patriarchal, and live in large joint families, with two or three sons and their families living together.

Tharus have their own spirit religion with their own priests, but in areas where they are in contact with Hindus, they have started worshiping some Hindu deities and hiring Brahmin priests for some ceremonies.

In the east, Tharus cremate their dead; in the west, they bury them.

Primarily farmers, their farming techniques remain primitive. Having lived apart for centuries, they are reluctant to change and join the world of those who have sought only to exploit them.

MOSLEMS IN NEPAL

Facing the temple of Akash Bhairab at Indrachowk in Kathmandu, behind a set of shops is a narrow alley with dozens of shops selling *pote*, the glass bead necklaces married Nepali women love so much. Many shopkeepers here are Moslem, descendants of Kashmiri traders who came here as long ago as the 15th century, at the invitation of the Malla kings.

In the hills north of Gorkha bazaar, the small hill bazaars sometimes echo with the call to prayer. More than two centuries ago the kings of the Chaubisi rajas brought in Moslem gunsmiths from India to train their people in the manufacture and use of guns. Their descendants are still here long after the kings and their kingdoms have disappeared.

These were small groups of migrants, who came for business and decided to stay. The first large wave of Moslem immigrants came as refugees following the unsuccessful Indian Mutiny of 1857. Most settled in the Terai as agricultural workers, others set up small businesses, some even continuing on into the southern Middle Hills.

Today most of Nepal's Moslem population live in the western

Terai. They are Sunni Moslems. They make up only about 3% of Nepal's total population, but are a majority in some areas of the west. Nepalgunj in the western Terai is said to be at least 70% Moslem.

Many Moslems speak Urdu as their first language. Many of them are farmers. In the large towns they also have small shops and businesses. They are also famous as *churate*, wandering all over the Middle Hills in the dry winters selling the glass bracelets called *chura,* that women like to wear.

Nepali Moslems have adopted some of the social stratification of their Hindu neighbors, based on occupation, with lower status given to those who practice the same types of jobs as the Hindu occupational castes do.

Women may live in a semi-*purdah*, and it is not uncommon to see women in the bazaar draped in black, their face hidden behind a black veil.

Moslems in Nepal follow the same rituals as Moslems everywhere, including Ramadan. Their biggest festival is Id at the conclusion of Ramadan.

INTERCASTE MARRIAGE

Marriage outside the limits of caste are still extremely rare. The custom of parents arranging their children's weddings has helped to keep this restriction strong. Family members who break this rule and marry outside their caste or group face strictures both social and religious.

Almost certainly they will be cut off by their family and lose their standing within the family. They will almost certainly be ostracized by the rest of the community as well: their action threatens not only their own families, but the system the whole community lives under.

Whoever has the higher caste of the two people involved will lose their caste. When the caste system was enforced by law, a man who associated with a woman from a caste higher than his own would be thrown in jail for violating her caste. These days both the man and woman would become social outcastes. They would probably try moving to a new area, perhaps taking on a new name, and keeping their mixed castes a secret.

Children of a mixed caste marriage are given the lower of their parents' castes. The case of children of a marriage between a caste Hindu and a person from a hill tribe is more complicated. A Brahmin man who married a Sherpa woman said his children were Chhetri. A caste woman who marries a Rai man, for example, would probably say her children are Rai as well.

THE CASTE SYSTEM AND YOU

Foreigners are in general treated as being outside the caste system. You will be welcomed in all but the most high caste, orthodox Brahmin homes. In some Brahmin homes you may just be given a seat on the porch. In no case will you be allowed into the kitchen area. If by mistake you touch the kitchen area, it is considered polluted and any food from it is jutho. It must be cleansed in a ceremony performed by the family priest.

The restrictions placed on you are no more than would be placed on any Nepali who came to the house and you should respect them whether you agree with them or not, just as any Nepali would.

When you entertain, remember that a Brahmin guest may not wish to eat rice prepared by you, and may turn down foods with garlic, onions, tomatoes, or chicken. Brahmins and Chhetris do not drink alcohol as well.

As more and more people travel abroad, some of the old prohibitions and restrictions are falling away, particularly in urban areas such as Kathmandu. Don't be surprised if your Brahmin guest asks for a beer, but then again don't be surprised if he turns down your offer of a beer and asks for a coke.

Status and Work

It's easy to see from even this very quick look at the caste system that Nepal is a structured, wondrously complex society. As bewildering as it is to foreigners, it is completely clear to Nepalis.

The caste system has made Nepali society very conscious of status and rank. Social encounters are rarely on the basis of equals. The people involved immediately establish some form of hierarchy, usually based on social standing, that decides the tone and manner of the encounter.

In almost any meeting, the determination of status and social rank is an important part of the preliminaries. Inquiries into name, hometown, and in the cities, job title and schooling help determine where each person fits into a meeting, and help people adjust their behavior accordingly.

LANGUAGES: NATIONAL AND OTHERS

Nepali, Nepal's official language, developed from the Sanskrit-based language of the ruling Brahmins and Chhetris. Nepal's government has made a concerted effort to make Nepali the true national language.

With the spread of education, radio, and the print media over the past 40-odd years, Nepali really has become the lingua franca of Nepal. Almost everyone in the country speaks some Nepali although in many areas the ability (particularly of the women) to use it may be very limited.

Nepali is the language of the home for about 50% of the population, but for the rest, it is only the public language: of the school, the office, and the market. In the home, babies still grow up learning their own group's language.

Today there are over a dozen major languages. Nepal's rugged, isolating geography further splits these languages into dialects so different that people in adjacent valleys may speak the same language, but have trouble understanding each other.

The second most commonly spoken language in Nepal is Maithili, the language of the east-central area of the Terai centered around Janakpur. Bhojpuri, the third most commonly spoken language, is the language of the central and western Terai from east of Birgunj to west of Bhairawa.

Both these languages, like Nepali itself, are Indo-Aryan languages related to Hindi and still further back to Sanskrit. Ultimately these languages share common roots with most European languages.

The languages of the hill tribes and Himalayan groups developed from an entirely different source and are grouped together as Tibeto-Burmese (sometimes called Sino-Tibetan). Think of Chinese, with its strings of syllables – each a word or idea – and its various intonations for a single syllable, to get an idea of how these languages work.

Somewhere in between is Newari, often called one of the most difficult languages in the world to learn. There is still some disagreement about its origins, but *People of Nepal* states that "although greatly influenced by Sanskrit, [Newari] is still distinctly a Tibeto-Burmese tongue."

– Chapter Three –

SADDHUS AND LAMAS

The great majority of Nepal's population are Hindu. There is a large Buddhist minority, mainly in the north, and a small Moslem minority, mostly in the southern Terai.

The 1981 census says the population is about 89% Hindu, 5% Buddhist, and 3% Moslem, with the remainder Jain, Christian, or 'other'. The figures for Hinduism are probably a little high and the figures for Buddhism a little low.

OVERLAP AND TOLERANCE

There is a great deal of overlap between Hinduism and Buddhism in Nepal, particularly in the Kathmandu Valley among the Newars.

Ask a Newar if they are Hindu or Buddhist and they'll probably smile and say, "Yes." Hindus consider the Buddha an avatar (incarnation) of the great Hindu god Vishnu. Buddhists think of the Hindu trinity of Brahma, Vishnu, and Shiva as different aspects of the earliest, original Buddha.

Differences between Hinduism and Buddhism become more pronounced in the Middle Hills and the Himalayas, where the religious traditions grew out of differing cultures. What does not change is the tolerance of one religion for the other.

This tolerance extended right up to Nepal's leadership. Usually strongly Hindu, Nepal's kings have never used their position to overtly advance Hinduism or suppress Buddhism. The Newar Malla kings in particular were evenhanded; building Hindu temples, but also maintaining and improving Buddhist centers like Swayambhu.

Another reason for the tolerance in Nepal may be that there is no centralized, organized religious hierarchy to voice objections or enforce a religious dogma to try and gain predominance.

Although they are rare, marriages between religions do occur, and almost certainly there are strong objections from one or both sides. A situation like that is largely treated as a family problem, though, not a community one. The problem is left to the families and individuals to solve.

RELIGION AND STATE

Under the Shah monarchy, Nepal proclaimed itself 'the only Hindu Kingdom in the world'. In spite of the Nepali people's strong tradition of religious tolerance, laws made it illegal for anyone to change their religion of birth and to proselytize.

These regulations fell particularly hard on the tiny group of Christians in Nepal. A number of Christians, including teenagers and children, were jailed for breaking the ban on proselytizing. The interim government freed these prisoners and stated it was in favor of complete religious freedom.

HINDUISM

Hinduism is a polytheistic religion that has its origins in the Indian subcontinent. It is considered the world's oldest living religion. It has had its ups and downs, but today it is the dominant religion of the subcontinent. It has been very influential as far away as Japan and its epic stories of the *Ramayana* and *Mahabharata* are popular throughout Southeast Asia.

Hindu philosophy is contained in a set of four massive volumes of scriptures called the *Vedas*, hymns first written down about 3,000 years ago. The portion called the *Upanishads* is concerned with the philosophy of Hinduism and obtaining knowledge of God, 'the knowledge that destroys the bonds of ignorance and leads to the supreme goal of freedom'.

Hinduism has such a vast set of scriptures full of so many ideas that it is impossible to pin down one set of beliefs. Hinduism encourages each of us to explore and make our own path, to adopt those beliefs out of Hinduism's vast pool of ideas that fit our needs.

People's Epics

Access to the dense, vast *Vedas* is restricted to the priestly Brahmin caste. To make the principles of Hinduism accessible to everyone, there are the *Mahabharata* and the *Ramayana*, two epic stories full of heroes and villains, virtue and evil, high adventure and romance.

Like the *Iliad* and *Odyssey*, they are based on true stories and events, embellished with fantastic deeds and the intervention of gods and goddesses. Although the stories are rooted in India, Nepal is mentioned in both.

The Mahabharata

The *Mahabharata* was first set down in the 4th or 5th century B.C. by Veda Vyasa, a scholar related to the protagonists, the Pandavas. It was added to until about the 4th century A.D. With 100,000 verses, it is one of the longest epics in the world.

Two royal clans of cousins feud for the throne of a kingdom. The throne rightfully belongs to the Pandava brothers: Arjuna, Bhima, Yudisthira, Nakula, and Sahadeva. Their father the king dies and leaves his brother, King Dhritarashtra, as regent until the Pandava sons come of age. Dhritarashtra, head of the Kaurava clan, has a hundred sons. As they grow up, the Kauravas become increasingly jealous of their Pandava cousins. When Dhritarashtra names Yudisthira as his heir, the Kauravas are furious.

By the time Yudisthira reaches the age of succession, Dhritarashtra's son Duryodhana persuades his father that he should have the throne. He convinces his father the Pandavas must be wiped out. The Pandavas discover the plot and escape to the great woods with their mother Kunti.

After wandering in the woods for some time, they hear news of an archery contest for the hand of the beautiful, virtuous Princess Draupadi. Arjuna enters the contest and wins. He rushes back and tells his mother he has won a great prize.

Kunti makes Arjuna promise that, as a good brother and faithful son, he will share his prize with his brothers. Unable to get a word of protest in, Arjuna reluctantly agrees, and Draupadi becomes the wife of all five brothers.

Meanwhile the Kauravas decide that it would be best to divide the kingdom in two and give half to their Pandava cousins. As soon as the Pandavas accept it and return, the Kauravas regret their compassion and Duryodhana starts plotting to get the Pandavas' half of the kingdom back.

He lures Yudisthira into a game of dice. Yudisthira loses everything: the entire Pandava kingdom and even Draupadi. Duryodhana and a brother immediately try to molest Draupadi; but the gods, mindful of her life-long piety, come to her aid and even enable her to demand the return of the Pandava kingdom.

But the Pandavas lose their kingdom again, and go in exile for 12 years. At the end of their exile, the Pandavas have built an army of friends and allies, and fight the Kauravas for the entire kingdom in the battle of Kurukshetra.

The Pandavas return to their kingdom and Yudisthira ascends the throne of the entire kingdom. The Pandavas' victory is a bitter-sweet one. Their mother Kunti is killed in a forest fire with Dhritarashtra. Yudisthira gives up his throne and leaves with his brothers and Draupadi on a long pilgrimage. They only find true peace when, after many ordeals and trials, they ascend to heaven.

The Ramayana

The *Ramayana* also originated in the 4th or 5th century B.C., and was added to over several centuries. It started as a secular entertainment for the royal courts, but became a religious epic as its hero Ramachandra, or just Ram, evolved into an incarnation of Vishnu.

The *Ramayana* is especially significant in Nepal because the home of Sita, daughter of King Janak and Ram's wife, is Janakpur, a Nepali town in the eastern Terai. Tribeni, south of Narayanghat, is another place identified with Sita as the home of her *guru* (teacher), where Sita and her children studied. Ruins still standing there are said to date from her time.

The story starts in far away Lanka (Sri Lanka) where King Ravana, a powerful demon, by practicing severe austerity, manages to induce Brahma into granting him a boon: Ravana cannot die at the hands of the deities or demons.

The gods soon realize what a mistake they've made, but Ravana has made one, too. As vain as he is evil, Ravana hasn't asked for protection from man.

The gods agree one of them must be reborn a mortal to destroy Ravana. The duty naturally falls on Vishnu the Preserver. He is born into the world dividing his nature between four sons born to King Dasaratha of different mothers: Ram gets half, Bharatha a quarter, and Lakshmana and Satrughna an eighth each.

On a trip with Lakshmana (his closest brother), Ram hears of a contest to win the hand of King Janak's beautiful daughter Sita. King Janak has in his possession Shiva's very own bow, and whoever can string the bow will win the hand of Sita.

Ram returns with his new bride. Dasaratha abdicates in favor of Ram, everything seems perfect, but where there is good, there is evil. A wicked servant of Bharatha's mother, Queen Kaikeyi, stirs up the queen to gain the throne for her own son.

Queen Kaikeyi tricks the unsuspecting King Dasaratha to agree to Bharatha's ascent to the throne and the banishment of Ram for 14 years. When he discovers what he has done, Dasaratha dies of grief within a week.

Ram, Sita, and Lakshmana leave for exile in a forest. Bharatha, who was away, is furious with his mother, and immediately goes to offer Ram his throne back.

Ram is duty-bound to honor his father's wish. Bharatha agrees to rule only as his regent, placing a pair of Ram's slippers on the throne as a symbol of the true king.

Meanwhile larger wheels are turning. Ravana's demoness sister Surpankha attempts to seduce Ram and Lakshmana, then attacks Sita when the brothers spurn her. Lakshmana defeats Surpankha, cutting off her nose, ears, and breasts.

Returning to her brother, she tells Ravana of Sita's astonishing beauty. Ravana wants Sita for himself. First he tricks Ram into leaving. Then he tricks Lakshmana, who is guarding Sita, to leave also, and tricks Sita into leaving a protective circle Lakshmana has drawn around her.

He carries Sita to Lanka in his sky chariot. Jatayu, an incarnation of Vishnu's eagle mount Garuda, sees Ravana and tries to stop him. Jatayu is mortally wounded in the fight, but lives long enough to tell Ram what happened.

Ram sets off to find Sita, along the way helping the monkey king Hanuman save his own kingdom. In return Hanuman becomes Ram's faithful ally.

Hanuman finds Sita in Lanka fighting off Ravana's advances and returns to tell Ram. After the monkey army builds a land bridge to Lanka, Ram finally confronts the demon and kills him.

By then the 14 years have past, and Ram and Sita return to their rightful throne.

The Mahabharata and Ramayana Today

The two epics remain as popular today as they ever were, a part of the popular literature and a continuing source of religious thought as well. Many children are named after the stories' heroes and heroines, and every child can tell you dozens of anecdotes that combine a good story and a moral.

Images from the stories illustrate the sides of houses in the Terai. Dozens of comic books (in English and Hindi) retell the stories for children. Made in India television series from the epics are the most popular shows in the country. They were also a reason for the TV boom in the Terai and the Kathmandu Valley.

The Self

The vast pantheon of gods and goddesses worshiped by Hindus are really different aspects of the one true God, Brahma, the 'Self' who is represented in the sound with no form, 'Om'.

The Self is found in everything and everyone: animals, rocks, trees, people. Hinduism's deities are manifestations of this one omnipresent force.

Merit, Rebirth, Release

Hindus believe in a cycle of life, death, and rebirth. All of us are striving to obtain *moksha* (release) from this cycle. There is a cosmic ladder to heaven, each rung another level of existence; everything from bugs and amoebas at the bottom to Brahmins at the top. Our souls move up and down this ladder with each rebirth we undergo. Ultimately we are trying to climb up and off the ladder, to liberation from this existence and entrance into heaven.

If your actions are good in this life, then in the next you move closer to moksha. If your actions are improper, if you disturb the harmony of your soul and the soul of others, then you will be punished in your next rebirth. Your soul will be placed in a lower form of existence.

Dharma (also called 'righteous living') is the set of principles for maintaining and enriching social, ethical, and spiritual harmony in life. The merit earned (or discarded) in this life by following (or rejecting) dharma determines your birth in your next life.

Hindu Gods and Goddesses

The various aspects of the single 'Om' are represented by the myriad gods and goddesses. At times they are full of divine wisdom and mercy, at others full of all the human emotions – even anger, envy, jealousy, and greed. They get drunk, quarrel, lust, just like humans.

The Hindu trinity consists of Brahma (the creator), Vishnu (the preserver), and Shiva (the destroyer).

Brahma created the cosmos and the other gods and goddesses. He is considered above everything and is hardly ever actively worshiped.

Vishnu is often called Narayan in Nepal. He is the protector and preserver. At different times he has found it necessary to come to earth to save mankind. To do this he takes on many avatars (forms) including the man-lion Narsingha. Hindus also consider Krishna, the blue-skinned cowherd-god and one of the main heroes of the *Mahabharata*; Ram, the hero of the *Ramayana*; and the Buddha as avatars of Vishnu. Vishnu travels on the back of Garuda, who is half-man, half-eagle.

It is an easy connection from Vishnu, the preserver and protector of mankind in various incarnations, to a king as preserver of his kingdom. The king of Nepal is traditionally considered to be an incarnation of Vishnu.

Shiva is by far the most popular god of Nepali Hindus, the god most often worshiped and appealed to. Within the Hindu trinity he is the destroyer, but he is also the recreator. He is Lord of Dance, joyous at the creative power of his steps; but as Bhairab he revels in the dance of destruction.

Shiva is most often depicted wrapped in a leopard skin, trident in one hand, an ash-smeared *saddhu* with the third, vertical eye of complete knowledge in his forehead. Even though he is a celibate saddhu, he also has a wife, Parbati, and children. Some of his most famous stories concern his drinking and carnal passions.

Shiva has over a thousand names. In Nepal he is often called Mahadev, the great god. His vehicle is the bull Nandi. A statue of

Shiva is the most worshiped god among Nepal's Hindus. He has thousands of names and manifestations. This small boy represents Shiva who, among other things, is Lord of Dance. The little girl is Shiva's wife Parbati.

Nandi kneeling is found outside almost every Shiva temple.

Inside the temple is the object of worship for Shiva, the *lingam*. A lingam is a naturally formed or sculpted stone pillar, the quintessential phallic symbol. Worshipers pour cow's milk over it, sprinkle it with flowers and red powder, offer fruits and sweets to it as signs of homage and supplication.

There are four paramount Shiva temples in the Hindu world, and the only one outside India is Pashupatinath, on the eastern outskirts of Kathmandu, in a sacred forest on the banks of the Bagmati River. (It is bordered by a golf course, and the international airport is nearby.) The present golden-roofed temple was built in 1696, but there has been a temple at this spot for centuries.

Ganesh, Shiva's son, is everybody's favorite and, after Shiva,

the most often worshiped god. It's hard not to like a god with an elephant head and a huge potbelly who loves to dance and is often depicted perched on his vehicle – a mouse. Ganesh is the god people make offerings to before they appeal to any other. He is the god of everyone from thieves to writers.

One of the most important and busy Ganesh shrines is tiny Ashok Binyak temple just northwest of Kasthmandap in the Hanuman Dokha area.

Saraswati is the wife of Brahma and the goddess of wisdom. She is depicted playing a sitar and riding a swan.

Laxmi is the wife of Vishnu and the goddess of wealth, beauty, and love. Like Venus, she is said to have risen from the foaming sea, seated on a lotus, and overwhelmed everyone with her beauty.

Durga is another form of Shiva's wife, Parbati. Fierce Durga is always portrayed as a multi-armed warrior sitting atop her tiger (sometimes lion) destroying the terrible demon Mahisasura, who threatened the world in the form of a water buffalo. The celebration of her victory is the basis for the most important festival of the Nepali year, Dasain.

The goddess Taleju, whom the Malla and Shah kings considered their special protectress, is another form of Durga. This makes Durga's victory all that more special to Nepalis.

Hanuman is the popular monkey god and friend of Ram, the hero of the *Ramayana*. His statues are usually draped in or painted red. The statue often has sweets pasted onto his mouth. Because of his devotion, sense of duty, and his martial abilities, he is especially important to the military and police.

Indra is the king of the heavens, ruling the community of gods and goddesses from his palace high atop Mt Meru. He is prominently featured in the *Vedas*.

Indra is also the god of rain (a rainbow is *indreni*, 'Indra's bow'). As god of rain he remains vitally important to farmers. Indra Jatra, the penultimate festival of the Kathmandu Valley, is eight days of celebrations dedicated to Indra, and the monsoon rains he graciously gives.

The Indra Jatra festival is a commemoration and celebration of the coming of the rains. Dancers in elaborate masks and costumes re-enact Indra's triumph over demons. A huge papier-mâché elephant, Indra's vehicle, careens through the streets, knocking down slow-movers to everyone's delight.

Hindu Worship

'Puja' is the word used to describe all acts of Hindu worship, whether it is the simple, quick act of a housewife at the household shrine or an elaborate, days-long worship by a Brahmin at a house or temple.

Elements of Hindu worship include colored powder (usually red), uncooked rice, flower petals, sweets, fruit, milk, yogurt, ghyu, fire, water, a bell, and sweet-smelling incense.

Each morning most households will perform some small personal worship at the family shrine or the local temple. The first footsteps heard on the early morning streets of Kathmandu are of people, usually women and girls, on their way to local temples. In their hands are small trays, usually copper, with a number of compartments.

In each compartment is an item used in the puja. Each is sprinkled in specified order over the image of the deity. This may be done by a young girl with no understanding of what she is doing or a pious old person who has done it thousands of times.

Animal Sacrifice

In more elaborate pujas, animal sacrifice is commonly performed: chickens, pigeons, goats, even water buffaloes may be sacrificed, either by beheading or cutting the throat. As they are sacrificed, their blood is used to consecrate an image of the god or goddess being worshiped, or to consecrate the object which the worshiper is asking the god to bless or protect.

Sometimes the blood of the slaughtered animal is used to give a tika to the worshipers. Once the animal has been sacrificed, a portion, usually the head, is presented to the god or goddess and the remainder is retained by the sacrificer.

Before an animal is sacrificed, the sacrificer will consult the animal and wait until it nods its head in acquiescence. Those which take too long are sprinkled with water to get them to nod, but if that doesn't work, the sacrifice may be delayed for five to 10 minutes as a group follows the animal around waiting for its approval.

Household Worship

Almost every home has its own household shrine, a small niche in the wall, a picture of a god or goddess in a corner or hung on the wall. Outside, there may be a small rock smeared with red powder, or the base of a small tree. In wealthier homes, there will be a small shrine constructed outside the house. Basil, called 'tulsi', is a sacred plant and you can find a planter filled with it in the courtyard of many upper caste Hindu homes (it is not used as a cooking spice).

Give and Take

In any form of puja there is an element of both giving and receiving. The god or goddess is worshiped and offerings are made. These offerings are called *naibedya* or *bheti*. The offerings are presented as the humble offering of a worshiper to the god.

Once offered, the naibedya is transformed. A small portion of the offering is returned to the giver, and this becomes an exalted boon, a blessing from the deity to its worshiper. This blessing is called *prasaad*.

When the woman of the house returns from her morning trip to the temple, she will give a small portion of the prasaad to each member of the household. Even though they did not take part in the puja, they benefit just as if they had worshiped personally. Worshiping acquires merit, but so does the receiving of prasaad. Each time you receive prasaad you gain merit toward your next rebirth.

Cows

The Hindu religion developed thousands of years ago from the pastoral traditions of Aryans crossing from the north into the sub-continent. Largely nomadic, they depended on their cattle for sustenance. Cows were a sign of wealth, and status.

Brahmins were paid (and are sometimes still paid) with a cow for performing their priestly duties. Over the centuries the cow became transformed into a sacred animal, the earthly embodiment of Laxmi, the goddess of wealth, and the 'earth mother' of us all.

During the Tihar festival dedicated to Laxmi, cows are worshiped with red tikas on their foreheads, flower garlands, and they are fed sweets and fruits. Worshipers will bow their forehead to her side, bow to her feet, and crawl under the cow's stomach.

In Nepal's past there were stiffer penalties for killing a cow than for killing some castes of people. Even today, hitting and killing a cow with a car could put the driver in jail for up to 20 years. That helps to explain why the cows feel free to sleep in the middle of busy city streets and why traffic is careful to avoid them.

But, when they go where they shouldn't or get into somebody's crops, people don't hesitate to give them a sound beating with sticks and stones that can make even non-Hindu onlookers wince.

Cows are perfect examples of how the divine and the banal are found in everything. It's a common sight in bazaars to see a cow getting its nose whacked for stealing a bunch of spinach from a vegetable seller while at the other end of the same cow a mother places her hand on the cow's side and then touches her baby's forehead and her own to obtain a blessing.

Because of the sacred nature of the cow, its natural by-products are often used in pujas. This means not only milk and yogurt, but even cow urine and dung.

The Hindu Temple

The characteristic form of Nepali Hindu temples is in the pagoda style. In the center of most temples is the god or goddess, who may be represented by a statue or a natural stone. A statue of the deity's 'vehicle', the animal the deity rides, is at the entrance of the temple.

Always walk around a temple clockwise, keeping your pure right side to the temple. Take off your shoes before entering. In major temples, non-Hindus will not be admitted to the inner part containing the deity. If you receive prasaad from a priest, you will be expected to make a token payment. You do not have to accept it if you don't want to.

BUDDHISM IN NEPAL

Nepal can truly say it is the home of Buddhism. Siddhartha Gautama, who became the Buddha, was born in present-day Nepal, in Lumbini near Bhairawa in the Terai about 563 B.C. Some of Buddhism's earliest and strongest communities were in Nepal. Today Nepal is one of the great centers of Tibetan Buddhism, both in the Kathmandu Valley and all across the northern Himalayan region.

Buddhism started to grow as the Buddha walked North India teaching. After his death in about 480 B.C., Buddhism grew quickly.

It got a big boost when Ashoka, the first great emperor of India, converted to Buddhism in 263 B.C. He made a pilgrimage to Lumbini and erected a still-standing pillar there to commemorate his visit. It is said he continued on to the Kathmandu Valley and built four large stupas to mark the cardinal points of the Buddhist community at what is now Patan.

There are several schools of Buddhism. The Hinayana (small boat) says that each individual must on his own achieve Nirvana and release from *samsara*, the cycle of life. Such a person is called an *arahat*. An arahat, having achieved Nirvana, spends his or her remaining time on earth teaching, then is released from samsara upon death.

In Mahayana (great boat), which spread north and east into Nepal, Tibet, and beyond, individuals who achieve Nirvana reject the chance to leave samsara and instead choose rebirth, in order to help others win their release. Such a person is called a Bodhisattva.

In Mahayana, compassion is considered one of the highest virtues. Avalokiteshvara, a central figure in Tibetan Buddhism, is considered the Bodhisattva of Compassion. The Dalai Lama is an incarnation of Avalokiteshvara.

Tibetan Buddhism: From Nepal and Back Again

In the first part of the 7th century, the great Tibetan King Tsrong-Tsong Gompo spread his empire over central Asia and even threatened China. The king of Nepal, Amsuvarman, perhaps fearing Tsrong-Tsong would start to look south too, sent his daughter Bhirkuti to become the king's bride. Bhirkuti was beautiful and a devoted Buddhist. As part of her wedding dowry she brought the Buddha's begging bowl and other Buddhist artifacts.

Tsrong-Tsong's second wife was a Chinese princess. She, too, was a firm Buddhist. Together, the two Buddhist princesses converted their ferocious husband to Buddhism. He in turn introduced Buddhism throughout Tibet.

At least that is the story. Today Bhirkuti is worshiped as the green Tara, the consort of Avalokiteshvara, the Buddhist Bodhisattva of Compassion.

The other major figure of Tibetan Buddhism is the great Tantric and teacher Padmasambhava (Guru Rinpoche) at the end of the 8th century. Tibetan Buddhism, with its strong Tantric influences, has been the religion of the Himalayan region ever since. The Tibetan Buddhist presence in Nepal has grown considerably with the influx of Tibetan refugees after the Chinese takeover in 1959.

The Buddha's Life

Lumbini, in the central Terai, is little more than a small pond bor-

The temple of Maya Devi marks the birthplace of the Buddha at Lumbini in Nepal's Terai. The foreground ruins are of monasteries built over a thousand years ago. In spite of its importance, Lumbini can only be reached with considerable effort and there are no facilities for tourists.

dered with brick. On its north side is a plain temple, Maya Devi, sheltered by a huge tree. This is the unpretentious birthplace of Siddhartha Gautama, better known by his appellation, the Buddha.

Mahayama, the Buddha's mother, gave birth to him on the spot where the temple stands today. She died shortly afterwards.

Suddhodana, Siddhartha's father, was a member of the royal family of Kappilvastu. He invited a holy man to foretell his son's future, and as soon as the holy man saw the baby, he prophesied Siddhartha's future.

Suddhodana wanted his son to be a warrior and ruler. He isolated the boy in a palace where all his wishes were met and everyone was young and healthy, reasoning that exposure to the hardships of life would turn Siddhartha towards religion.

Siddhartha grew into a fine young man unspoiled by the luxury surrounding him, intelligent, kind, sensitive, athletic, and a skilled warrior. At the age of 16, he married beautiful Yashodhara, defeating her other suitors in a series of contests.

With his intelligent inquiring mind, Siddhartha became curious about life outside his beautiful palaces. He enlisted the help of his groom Channa and secretly made three trips outside the palace. For the first time Siddhartha saw what every person's fate is. On the first trip he saw an old man, on the second a sick man, and on the third a corpse.

The shock did not frighten him, but it did concentrate his attention on the larger questions of life. After considerable thought, he became determined to go outside again.

On this trip, he and Channa met a saddhu. Dressed in rags, with no possessions, home, or family, the saddhu still radiated serenity and tranquility. Siddhartha realized that to truly understand the saddhu's serenity, he would have to take the saddhu's path. He was wretched because of his love for his father and wife (and their soon-to-be-born child), but a stronger force pulled him away. On midnight of the very day his son was born, Siddhartha left his palace for the last time.

By the side of a river, he had his hair cut off roughly. He gave a saddhu his silken robe in exchange for the saddhu's rags. Then he gave his jewelry and horse to Channa, said goodbye, and walked off alone on his spiritual quest.

He studied with great teachers and increased his intellect and knowledge, but still was not satisfied. Then he set off to live deep in a jungle, depriving himself of everything, reasoning that by extreme suffering, his answers could be found.

His asceticism was so impressive he gained five disciples, but he himself didn't feel he was getting closer to what he was searching for. Realizing that he'd starve to death before he found them, he started to eat small amounts of food again.

His disciples deserted him, disgusted with his softness, but Siddhartha felt he had found the way that was right for him. Having experienced total sensual indulgence and total asceticism, he determined to attempt to find his answers by a middle way between these two extremes.

At Bodh Gaya in North India, he made a cushion of tree branches and sat under a Bodhi tree, determined to find his answers or die trying. Mara, a sort of Buddhist Satan, came to tempt him.

Through *vipassana*, a meditation technique, he became more and more aware until his perception of his own being and the world around him changed completely. He went beyond the boundaries of his own ego to experience the world as a unity.

When he ended his meditation, he saw the world with a clarity he had never known before. He was no longer Siddhartha. He was the 'Buddha', the enlightened one.

It had taken the Buddha six years of arduous work to reach enlightenment. For the next 45 years he walked North India and Nepal teaching, perhaps even reaching Kathmandu. During this time the Buddha converted hundreds of people to be *bhikkhus* (monks) and *bhikkunis* (nuns).

At first the Buddha instructed the bhikkhus and bhikkunis to continually wander and teach, but the realities of monsoon weather in North India eventually persuaded him to change his view.

Traveling in the monsoon is difficult and unpleasant. It is also the time of renewing life, with a rush of new plants and animals appearing. Partly to save his bhikkhus from monsoon travel, partly to avoid trampling or harming this new life, the Buddha organized 'rain retreats': places where monks could gather together and pass the monsoon. These gradually became year-round centers for Buddhist study, the monasteries of today.

At the age of 80, the Buddha died after eating a meal prepared by a smith named Cunda. After his death he passed directly into Nirvana, the ultimate heaven.

Only after his death were the Buddha's words recorded, so everything is secondhand. He based his teaching on a simple set of four axioms.

The Four Truths
The basic tenets of Buddhism are the Four Truths:
1. In this world there is suffering (*dukkha*). Suffering is both physical and mental. But the existence of suffering does not mean there is no happiness (*sukkha*) in the world.

2. There is a cause for all suffering: it is desire, not only the desire for material wealth and sensual pleasure. Even someone who wishes to do good deeds is expressing a desire. Desires are what propel us on the wheel of life, taking us from one moment, from one life, to the next.

3. Suffering can be ended by releasing ourselves from our desires. We can end our suffering and desires and even take a path that leads us right off the wheel of life to the condition called Nirvana, a sort of heaven.

4. There is a method for ending suffering. There are practical steps which will enable us to leave behind our desires and lead us toward Nirvana. These steps are the Eightfold Path.

The Eightfold Path
1. Right Understanding
2. Right Thought
3. Right Speech
4. Right Action
5. Right Livelihood
6. Right Effort
7. Right Mindfulness
8. Right Concentration

The steps of the eightfold path are grouped into three sections:
1. Wisdom: Right Understanding and Thought are grouped together as wisdom. Understanding is not blind faith in the Buddha's words, but it comes from carefully considering his words and testing them against our own experience. Right Thought refers to motivation and the direction of our thoughts. There should be no expectation of personal gain, of new powers or wealth. Right Thought means focusing our attention, concentrating with the idea not of what we can gain, but how we can help the wider world.

2. Morality: Right Speech, Action, Livelihood, and Effort. Right Speech involves putting an end to swearing, harsh language, slander, backbiting, boasting, and lying. Right Action includes not stealing and not taking life of any kind. It is all right to eat meat only if the animal was not killed specifically to provide you with meat. Moderation of the senses also covers the mind and the body. Drinking and drugs is another subject incorporated in Right Action. Right Livelihood, in our complex modern

world, might best be expressed as that our profession should cause no harm. In Right Effort, Buddhism recognizes there must be effort in this world; passivity is not enough. To be aware, perceptive, and sensitive requires effort.

3. Meditation is Right Mindfulness and Right Concentration. Meditation is too complex to go into here. Concentration is setting aside all distractions, both external and in our mind, enabling us to see with greater clarity.

The Wheel on The Cart

Both Hinduism and Buddhism include the concept of Karma. Karma refers to the willed actions of the mind, body, and speech. All actions have consequences, both for the person who does the action and whomever the action is directed at. Good actions grow into good consequences. A person who leads a good life full of good Karma will eventually reap the benefits, either in this life or the next. A person's bad Karma will just as surely lead to bad consequences.

Tantra

A powerful force in both Hinduism and Buddhism in Nepal is Tantrism. The practices of Tantrism originated in India, in the Hindu *Vedas* and *Upanishads*.

In Tantrism, the cosmic forces and the energies of an individual, all things and every action, are intertwined. A *tantra* is a scripture (it may be recited, written, or visualized) which allows the Tantric (the person utilizing it) to unleash enormous energy and reach an altered state of consciousness. Stories of Tibetan monks levitating or flying are examples of harnessing this Tantric power.

To use a tantra, a person must be initiated properly and trained by a guru. Different people have different levels of receptiveness, and the guru must determine how far his student may go.

The Tantric uses two main tools. One is his *mandala*, a drawing symbolizing both the cosmos and a human being, a map of the Tantric's spiritual journey and psychic potential. The second main tool is the *mantra*, of which there are two types. The *bija mantra*, the seed mantra, is a single sound which incorporates the essence of a specific Tantric deity. Visualized, written down, or recited, a mantra frees the mind of clutter and helps focus the mind as it searches for the path to enlightenment. The Tantric's mantra is a passage, usually of sanskrit origin. To the properly trained user, his mantra crackles with potential energy.

The most well-known, frequently heard mantra is 'Om Mane Padme Hum'. Translated as 'Hail to the Jewel in the Lotus', this mantra is carved onto rocks and cliffs, painted on walls, printed on prayer flags, placed inside prayer wheels, and is constantly on the lips of people.

Tantrism puts great emphasis on action, ritual, and true experience. One direction some Tantrics have taken is using sex to unleash Tantric power. In Hinduism this is represented often by the union of Shiva with his *shakti* (power), his female counterpart. In Buddhism it is deities like Chandamaharoshan and his female counterpart, Chakra Samvara.

Symbols and Motion as Prayer

Symbols of the people's strong Buddhist faith fill the hillsides, trails, and villages. Strings of thin cotton flags flap in the cold breezes that never seem to die. The flags are printed with Buddhist prayers, each wave of the flag in the wind sends the prayer to heaven again, earning the person who put up the flag more merit for the trip to heaven.

Mane wheels, cylinders with a mantra or prayer placed inside, also depend on motion to carry their unspoken prayers to heaven. Some sit in small houses over a stream, a water wheel spinning them constantly.

Prayer flags on the homes of a high village in the Himalayas send Buddhist prayers to heaven each time they flap in the breeze.

Others are set in rows in a wall along the trail. As people walk by (keeping to the left) they give the wheel a spin, earning merit for themselves and for the person who installed the wheels.

Smaller mane wheels are carried by people. A counter-weight and a flick of the wrist keeps the wheel and the mantra inside spinning as the people walk or talk to friends – praying and gossiping at the same time.

Chapter Four

THE NEPALI LIFE CYCLE

Discussing the Nepali life cycle is obviously a problem. There are so many diverse groups it's best to remember that generalizations are just that – generalizations, and you should not be surprised when you find a person or group of people saying or doing something different.

The Nepali life cycle is based on the four stages of Hinduism's traditional life cycle:

- Childhood: care-free and fun
- Student-hood: a time for diligent study, developing character and discipline
- Adulthood: devoted to service to parents, children, and work
- Old age: a time to relax, pray and meditate

A good education (academic, that is) is still beyond most children in Nepal, but the principles of the Hindu life cycle are easily seen throughout Nepali society.

Boys vs. Girls

Nepalis love any baby that's not theirs. But for themselves, most parents will tell you the more boys the better; just spare us the girls.

Boy babies mean another worker, another support for the parents in their old age, another son to conduct the all important funeral rites for them.

The birth of a girl means more responsibilities and expenses for the parents. They have to be protected until they are married, and then there is the sometimes arduous task of finding a suitable husband, agreeing on a dowry, and the heavy burden of the wedding expenses to be borne. A daughter provides work while she is at home, but her labor is lost when she marries and joins her husband's household.

Childbirth

Women will keep working almost right up to the time they go into labor. Medical care is almost non-existent throughout most of Nepal, and pre-natal care is still unknown.

The birth of the child is usually attended by the community midwife called a *sudeni*. Hygiene is poor during childbirth. The knife or scissors used to cut the umbilical cord are hardly ever sterilized or even cleaned. Oil, ghyu, even cow dung are applied after cutting the umbilical cord.

Starting Out

Brahmin and Chhetri castes consider both the mother and newborn child untouchable for 11 days. At least this means the mother can rest from most of her normal work.

On the 11th day a purification and name-giving ceremony takes place. The name is chosen by an astrologer based on the postion of the planets and stars at the exact moment of birth.

Many hill tribes have a similar name-giving festival, with Buddhists consulting a lama to determine the name. Hill tribes will give extra food, especially meat, to a woman who has just given birth, if they can afford to. Usually this is a chicken cooked soon after childbirth specifically for the new mother.

Oil Massages

Walking anywhere in Nepal you will see mothers sitting outside, massaging their babies from head to toe with mustard oil. Almost all communities in Nepal share this custom. It's considered an essential part of the baby's post-natal care and is given daily.

Pasni

The next event in a person's life is *pasni*, the rice-feeding ceremony, when the infant is around six months old. All the relatives are invited for this important ceremony. Family friends may be invited, too. Guests give presents (clothes, food, money) to the baby. A Brahmin or lama presides over the feeding of rice to the infant.

While pasni marks the start of the weaning process, it is not uncommon for a child to continue to be breast fed until they are two years old or more.

Infancy

Wrapped around the waist of most women in Nepal is a long piece of cloth called a *patuka*. At times a wallet, tool kit, even lunchbucket, mothers use it to strap their baby on piggyback. The infant is constantly with its mother: in the fields, doing the cooking, washing clothes. Perched on its mother's back, the baby is introduced to every facet of its new world.

When a child starts walking, it is turned over to an older sibling or relative for its daycare. This is usually a sister, who may be only a few years older. Nepal's high birthrate guarantees there is no shortage of other children for the child to play with, either in its own household or around the village.

Early Health

The infant mortality rate in Nepal is one of the highest in the world. UNICEF statistics state 11 out every 100 babies die before they reach their first birthday, and a survey by New ERA found 40% of these die within four weeks of birth. Mortality rates continue to be high up to the age of five. The mortality rate for all children up to five years of age is 16.5%. If a child can reach the age of five, their chances of reaching adulthood improve dramatically.

Diarrheal diseases are the main cause of infant mortality. Toilet training by parents starts as soon as the baby can walk. As long as the child cannot clean itself, this is done by the parents.

Toddlers are taught to at least go out on the porch to urinate, and to defecate beside a nearby path, in a nearby garden or field, or near a water source. Water sources are also a favorite place for children to play. Children are taught to clean themselves with their left hand after defecating, but are very seldom taught to clean their hands after.

Childhood

In general a child is treated with indulgence and permissiveness. Discipline around the house is loose. Physical punishment is often threatened (with small children in a joking manner), but rarely inflicted. Most discipline stops with a verbal reprimand. Much of a child's social skills and education comes from interaction with older siblings and other children.

There are few toys available: children fashion their own out of whatever they can find. Rolling hoops is a favorite everywhere. Kite flying (and kite fighting) during the spring and around the Dasain holiday in the autumn is a national pastime.

This merry-go-round is powered by the boy pulling the arms of the carousel while his boss, an adult, hustles up more business. Child labor is normal in Nepal, even though there are labor laws against most forms of child labor.

Girls play a jacks-like game using a handful of small rocks. Monsoon-swollen irrigation ditches become play rivers and makeshift swimming pools.

By the time a child is five or so, they will have to start taking responsibilities. There will probably be a younger sibling to watch over. Girls in particular will be given various domestic chores to perform on their own or they will be made to help adults. Common jobs for children from five onward include fetching water, firewood, and fodder.

In most homes children eat only after the older male members of the household have eaten. If a child is hungry and protests, it is then allowed to eat with them. The male members of the family get first choice on food, and male children usually are given the best of any food available to children. Malnutrition is a common problem, especially in the months preceding and at the start of the monsoon, when food is traditionally in short supply.

Chudakarma

At the age of six or seven, Hindu boys undergo an important ceremony called *chudakarma* or *kshyaur*. It is an initiation ceremony which establishes the boy's identity as a Hindu. During the ceremony, the boy's head is shaved except for a small tuft called a *tupi*. The tupi marks the boy as a Hindu. Only the boy's mother's brother may preside at this ceremony, and if she has none, a cousin is asked.

Approaching Adolescence

As children approach adolescence, the ratio of their playtime to worktime gradually reverses as they learn what their adult responsibilities will be and take more of them on.

In the rural areas, firewood and fodder collection are common jobs for children. Trips to the forest are made with a group of other children. At this (and other communal work situations) children see and discuss everything in their world. In areas where the forests are an hour's walk or more away, the children may be away the better part of the day.

Another job commonly given to children is grazing the livestock, anything from dozens of goats to a couple of water buffaloes. Grazing livestock is a job with a lot of 'down time' and there is plenty of opportunity to play with other grazers, talk about things, or simply watch the clouds go by.

If a child is lucky enough to go to school, the school day starts at about 10 a.m. and finishes by mid-afternoon. Schools may be an hour's walk or more from home. Schools are usually built at the top of hills or ridges.

Usually boys will be allowed to go to school. Girls go to fetch water, graze the livestock and generally help around the house.

Adolescence and on to Adulthood

By the time adolescence comes, most girls have left school and taken on an almost fulltime work load. The percentage of boys enrolled in school also drops, but not as much as that of girls.

The onset of puberty is treated differently by Hindus and Buddists, both in how society marks it and what meaning is given to it. And with Hindus there is a great difference between the treatment of girls and boys.

Hindu Daughters: Tough Changes

A Brahmin or Chhetri daughter is taken to a room in another house at the onset of her first menses and kept isolated for two weeks. She is considered so polluted during this time she is forbidden even sight contact with male relatives. Women who bring her food and water and keep her company will avoid her touch.

From then on, she will have to stay isolated from her family for the first four days of every menses. During this time she must not take part in any food preparation. She must avoid contact with any man who wears the janai, including her own husband and sons.

With the onset of the menstrual cycle, the girl becomes a woman. Her relationship with her parents and brothers and all other men is changed. Physically, the horseplay and even casual contact between brother and sister will end: the sister becomes 'sacred'. Her safety, welfare, and purity are major obligations her parents and brothers must fulfill.

Women become extremely shy and timid when in the company of even familiar men and positively tongue-tied in the presence of strangers.

A heavy burden now weighs on the parents, particularly the father. The daughter is as sacred as a cow. The father successfully completes his responsibility to his daughter by getting her married. Marrying off a daughter earns the parents a great deal of religious merit and considerably helps their chances of entering heaven.

A daughter whose purity is lost (by relations with men before marriage) is considered unmarriageable. The parents have failed in their responsibility. They are disgraced in the community and lose the merit they could have aquired from a *kanya* (pure) daughter. So though the daughter is sacred, it is a very fragile and worrisome sanctity.

Naturally the chances for pollution are thought to be greater the older the woman is. There is heavy pressure on the parents to complete the duty as quickly as possible, even before the onset of puberty. Until recently child marriages were common, with a bride of six bringing the most merit to the parents.

Sidestepping The Question

Newars escape the traumas of the obligations of marriage by marrying their daughters at about the age of seven to the god Narayan (Vishnu) in the form of a bel fruit (areca nut).

The wedding is a full wedding ceremony: the bride wears a red sari, and gold ornaments, and *sindoor*, the red tika powder, is placed in the parting of her hair.

By marrying a god, any later marriages by the girl are reduced to secondary status. This ceremony helps to ease everyone around some thorny religious and cultural issues. The marriage to the bel fruit sees to it that the girl is married with full rites, which is very important. Divorce after full marriage rites is impossible; since she marries her human husband with only partial rites, then divorce is possible.

It also makes it possible for a widow to remarry. Possible, but both divorce and remarriage of divorcees and widows is still rare in Newari culture.

Hill Tribe Daughters

Daughters in hill tribe societies do not face the same restrictions and fears as caste Hindu daughters do, and their parents do not have the same trepidations as Hindu parents do. As there is no heavy sense of religious obligation tied to the marriage of daughters, the attitude toward puberty and relations with men is not as sensitive.

In contrast to the extreme shyness of caste Hindu teenage girls, teenage girls of many hill tribes are happy to answer questions from strange men and even flirt if they like. Rough-housing between teenage boys and girls is normal.

With no taboos about purity at marriage, premarital relationships are an accepted (but not encouraged) part of growing up. Most hill tribe cultures even have a mechanism for allowing contact between teenagers. The Gurung rodi is a good example.

Boys: Passing into Manhood

Most groups have some celebration or ceremony to mark the attainment of manhood for boys. High caste Hindus call the ceremony bratabandha or *upanayana*. During this elaborate ceremony the boy receives his janai (sacred thread) for the first time. After receiving the thread, the boy is considered to have taken a major step toward adulthood and is given additional responsibilities. The boy is now eligible to eat with the men of the house. The bratabandha ceremony takes place when the boy is eight or so for Brahmins and at a later age for Chhetris.

The considerable cost of staging a bratabandha ceremony can be a severe burden on poorer households. A group ceremony for 20 or more boys helps to ease the expense.

Hindu Newars also have bratabandha ceremonies. Buddhist Newars have a similar ceremony. The boys are not given a janai, but have a ritual bath and their heads are shaved. Draped in saffron robes, they relive the life of the Buddha in a day, carrying a begging bowl from house to house. Usually the begging route is carefully planned and the boys are accompanied with considerable fanfare.

Hill tribes have their own customs. Gurungs, for example, have a ceremony for sons at two years of age called *putpute,* during which the boys of the village dance at the home of the baby. Brothers and relatives give presents to the child. When a boy reaches five or six, a celebration is held following a ceremony to mark his first formal haircut.

COURTSHIP
Hindus

When the caste Hindu woman crosses the line from childhood to sexual maturity, casual conversation with males older than herself comes to an end. Hindu society has few opportunities for social relationships between teenagers of opposite sex.

Parents do not encourage their daughters to meet or talk to boys either, fearful that something might happen that could make it difficult or impossible for them to arrange a marriage and thereby fufill their responsibility as parents.

Hill Tribes

Contact between teenagers in the hill tribes and the Himalayan societies is much more free and open. Teenagers are free to mix, flirt and experience romances.

Many types of work in the village are done communally. Large groups of people will go together to the forest to collect firewood and fodder. Young people get to know each other in a relaxed, casual manner through these activities. Trips to the forest in particular offer a great opportunity to have more private conversations.

With the Himalayan groups in particular, young lovers engage in wrestling that would put some professional wrestlers to shame. Arm twists, thumps to the head, even bloody noses can be a part of 'getting to know each other'.

Singing for A Bride

Most villages hold a *mela*, a fair lasting up to several nights, during the year. These draw young people from neighboring villages

together. The mela is a great chance to see new faces, or see old faces in a new way.

A favorite activity then is an informal singing contest. Under a large tree or *chautaraa*, a group of boys faces a group of girls (in the east Rais and Limbus hold hands and slowly dance in a circle – boys and girls together – as they sing). The two groups take turns to sing improvised verses to a simple melody. The verse is a quick reply to the preceding verse of the other side.

A premium is placed on verses that reply with wit, making a humorous, cutting remark about the other side. Singers come and go as the evening unfolds and the singing can go on all night.

During the course of the singing a boy may (indirectly) sing to a particular girl on the other side. If she wants to return his interest, she does so in her reply. The boy and girl can in this way engage in a singing contest during the course of which they arrange to meet later in the evening. Or they may just slip away from the contest and go off together privately. Romance and marriage may well result from a song.

MARRIAGE

Marriage is almost universal in Nepal. Hindu religion places such great importance on marriage that well over 90% of the population marry. Monogamous marriage is the most common form throughout Nepal, but polygamy (one man to several women) and polyandry (several men to one woman) are also practiced.

Polygamy

The National Code of 1963 makes bigamy a punishable offense under the law, but another provision secures the right of the man to continue his lineage due to the importance of the son in Hindu religion. The law allows a man to take another wife if his marriage has no living children after 10 years. In common practice a man may take another wife to obtain the male heir he needs, but the second wife may just be a sign of his wealth or vanity. This has been an accepted part of Hindu culture for centuries.

Given the paucity of a woman's rights under Nepali law and custom, acceptance of another wife is often preferrable to divorce (see *Divorce*).

Polyandry

Polyandrous marriage in Nepal is practiced by the Himalayan groups. The reason for Hindu polygamy can be found in religion, but the reason for polyandrous marriage among Himalayan peoples is cultural. A polyandrous marriage prevents the necessity of splitting the household's limited resources among brothers setting up their own households. Also, men may be on the road for several months or even a year at a time trading and traveling. A polyandrous marriage means that there will always be one man around to help in the household.

Most polyandrous marriages involve two brothers and one wife. If there are three brothers in a family, generally one of them will become a monk. Households with more than two brothers in the house are uncommon.

Any children born of this type of marriage are recognized as the child of the eldest brother, no matter who the biological father is.

Arranged Marriages

The responsibility for marriage among Hindus falls on the parents, most heavily on the father of the girl. Pre-marital sexual experience is excused in boys, but no allowances are made for a woman, and her sexual purity is imperative. The act of the parents giving their daughter is called *kanyadan,* 'kanya' meaning virgin.

Prime importance is attached to the fact that the bride is kanya. A woman can only truly marry while she is pure. A divorced or widowed woman is no longer pure; marriage to her would pollute the man, decrease his purity, and put his next life in jeopardy.

Kanyadan (giving a virgin in marriage) earns the parents a great deal of merit. To fail in arranging a daughter's marriage (or to fail to keep the daughter pure until marriage) is a disgrace and can hurt the parents in their next life.

The groom must come from within the same caste, as a marriage to a lower caste would be a disgrace and result in loss of caste for the girl. Finding a suitable groom of the right caste and right background can sometimes be difficult, taking months or years.

The marriage negotiations are not conducted directly between the parents. A *lami* (go-between), usually a relative of the girl, conducts the marriage negotiations. It is usually the girl's parents who initiate the search and negotiations.

Background checks are made and, in some cases, the bride's dowry and/or *tilak* (bride price) must be agreed upon.

The girl and boy may or may not know that the negotiations are taking place. These days, before the negotiations are completed, a photo of the prospective spouse may be shown to the boy and girl and a general description given. The young people will be asked for their assent. In Nepali law and custom, they must consent to their parents' arrangement, but a dutiful son or daughter would be reluctant to oppose their parents.

In urban areas a discreet, casual meeting may be arranged within a larger social gathering. The boy and girl may not even speak, but at least they get a chance to see each other in a social situation.

Child Marriage

Nepalis in general marry while young. One survey showed that only 2.4% of women get married after reaching 25.

The pressure on both parents and daughter that she be pure at the time of marriage makes marriage at an early age very attractive.

Child marriage was accepted, even encouraged in Hindu culture. Six years old was deemed the age at which the parents would gain maximum merit for the wedding. The wedding takes place, then the children return to their homes until they reach puberty.

The National Code of 1963 completely banned child marriage. No girl before the age of 14 can be married. A marriage is also declared null if either the boy or girl does not consent to it when they reach the age of 16.

Another law forbids marriage if the man is more than 20 years older than the female. The law makes the marriage punishable, but does not automatically annul it, making it difficult for an orthodox Hindu family to find their daughter a second bridegroom.

The traditions of society and sanctions of religion are powerful forces. Child marriage continues to be a problem, mostly in the Terai. One 1981 survey found that 22.5% of the female population were married before reaching 15.

Choices

Each hill tribe is further sub-divided into *thars* (clans) and there may be restrictions concerning marriage within the thar or what other thars the marriage may occur with.

The Kiratis forbid marriage between cousins, but among the Gurungs, Magars, Thakalis, and Tamangs of central Nepal, marriage with a cousin is preferred.

Arranged marriages are prevalent among well-to-do families or in areas in close contact with high caste Hindus. In the hill tribes, it is the boy's father who usually initiates negotiations with a girl's family.

Again, a go-between is used, in this case a relative of the boy. In many cases the acceptance by the girl's parents of an offering of raksi by the go-between signifies acceptance of the wedding offer.

By Capture

A boy may choose to capture his bride. He may do this with or without the girl's knowledge and cooperation.

He may kidnap her during the festivities and distractions of a mela, or simply grab her when she goes off to fetch water or collect firewood.

He takes her to the home of a relative rather than his own home. He then has three days to convince her to become his wife. If she still refuses, she is free to return to her own home. If she accepts, a regular wedding ceremony is held (after her parents have been placated). If the girl's parents are really upset, they may approach the boy's house. The boy's parents must calm them down before the courtship can continue.

A boy and girl may simply elope to avoid the time and expense of arranging a wedding or to overcome their parents' objections. Once the parents are reconciled, the ceremonies may be held.

Free Choice

The Himalayan cultures are free to choose their own spouse, and the lack of restrictions on social contact between the sexes makes this easy. However, there are some restrictions on marriage between different clans within Sherpa society.

Richer families may arrange marriages, and most polyandrous marriages also take place by arrangement within rich households.

ADULTERY

Adultery is a religious sin and a civil offense for both parties, but traditionally it has been the women who get the blame and most of the penalties. In Hindu religion, the man can purify himself of the sin by a ritual bath. A woman cannot regain her purity by any means and remains polluted for the rest of her life.

Under the old civil codes the penalties for adultery depended on the caste of the two people involved, with the most severe punishments meted out for an adulterous relationship between a low caste man and a high caste woman.

The man had to pay a sum of money to the husband of the woman, depending on caste and status. The woman's marriage was dissolved and she was considered the wife of the man she had committed adultery with. The woman was treated as little more than a piece of property.

Under present law, a payment of Rs 2,000 must be made. The man and woman must both go to prison for two months, and the woman is considered the wife of the man she commits adultery with.

For this to happen, though, the woman's husband must bring the case to court. That leaves an opening for traditional practices to deal with the situation. Tamangs, for example, have a practice whereby the man must pay the husband of the woman a fine. The relationship of the people involved is up to them to decide. The husband and wife may even decide to reunite.

OLD AGE

Although life expectancy in Nepal is in the mid-40s, the greatest mortality rate is in the youngest years. So if a person lives to be five, they stand a good chance of reaching old age. There is no shortage of elderly people.

As their children grow, marry, and start to raise families of their own, it's time for the parents (now grandparents) to relax a little. Most people remain active and work as long as they are able. When they are no longer able to work in the fields, old people work around the house, watch the grandchildren, sit in the sun, offer advice. The elderly are active members of their family and community.

There are no nursing homes, no seniors' communities, no special programs to care for the elderly. A very strong sense of duty remains that the eldest son should care for his parents as they become unable to support themselves.

Education

Non-formal education comes largely from other children. Pre-schools are increasingly popular in urban areas, but these are mainly concerned with teaching specific information (the alphabet, for example) rather than thinking or learning processes.

Education is a dilemma for parents. Most want to see their children educated, but most families need all the help they can with farming and domestic work. In spite of incentives from the government, education still costs money and even small sums can be a burden for many households.

Most households will make the effort to send at least one child to school. Usually that child is a boy. A reasonable estimate is 51% of boys and 29% of girls between the ages of six and nine are enrolled in school. Girls are more likely to drop out of school than boys.

When the Rana era ended in the early 1950s, about 5% of the population could read and write. The Nepali government made education a top priority. Schools and school enrolment increased dramatically. Recently the rates of increase have slowed down and in some areas rates have even started to decline. One reason is parents cannot see any benefits to education. The upward economic mobility education was said to guarantee has not come about.

Schools are small, damp, poorly furnished, badly lit, and crowded. It is not uncommon for 40 or 50 students to be in one class. Many classes are held outside on the grass. Many schools have no benches or desks. Textbooks are free from the government, but these are often in short supply.

Teachers are underpaid and under-motivated. The traditonal learning and teaching method is rote memorization, and that is still the case. Little emphasis is placed on applying knowledge or developing a line of thought. Discipline is tight compared to the home.

Chapter Five

NEPALI WAYS OF SEEING

STATUS: A DETERMINING FACTOR

Ijjat, meaning prestige with shadings of status, honor, and self-respect, is an important concept in human interactions in Nepal. The working relationships between people, the conversation of people who meet on the street, are rarely that of equals. In the interaction of two people, one is higher than the other.

That's true both inside the family and outside, in public and in private. It is expressed not only in the way people talk, but in the very words they use. The various forms of 'you' convey different degrees of status or prestige.

Fluid Status

A person does not have the same prestige in every situation. Status is fluid, determined by the people involved at that moment. A person's status may change as a new person enters the conversation or one leaves it.

A section chief may be a tiger one moment, yelling at every staff in sight, and suddenly become as meek as a lamb when his boss comes in the office. No one doubts the tiger will return as soon as the boss leaves the office again.

Traditional factors for determining status are sex, age, caste, education, occupation, and wealth. In the urban areas, particularly the 'development circle' of government and development agencies of Kathmandu, factors like job title, salary, and university degrees are also important.

The observation of status, the conference of proper ijjat when talking or working with someone, is an important part of all human interactions in Nepal.

Status within The Family

In Hindu, Newar, and many hill tribe cultures, joint and extended families are the norm. A joint household consists of two or more married men in the same household. They may be father and son(s) or brothers. An extended family includes family members outside the nuclear family (a widowed mother, an unmarried or divorced brother or sister, for example).

Nuclear families are becoming more common in the ever expanding government service and development-related populations. Often the fathers in these families leave their families in Kathmandu or send them home while they work in the field and work for a transfer back to Kathmandu.

Within the family, age and sex are the two main determinants. Nepal is a patriarchal society. The degree varies from group to group, but the last word in almost every family is the father's.

At the head of the household is the oldest male. If the oldest male becomes unable to make decisions, the next oldest male becomes the *de facto* head of the household, with the oldest member as the ceremonial head.

The division of power is less clear in many hill tribe families. There is more power sharing between men and women than in caste Hindu families.

Husbands and Wives

Between husband and wife there is public status and private status. In public, women rarely speak out at all, let alone challenge a man. Public meetings in Nepal are usually all male affairs. Women may be working within earshot, but they will rarely interrupt their work to actually take part in the discussion.

In the privacy of her own home, though, a woman will make her thoughts known on the topic of discussion, often quite forcefully.

The pitiful economics of farming in Nepal often necessitate the man leaving home to find work. He may travel to the Terai, join the army or police, the Indian Army, the British Army, or simply travel to India to look for seasonal work. During this time the woman will be in sole charge of all aspects of the farm.

The man may be away for months and often years at a time. The woman becomes experienced and adept at running the household and, when the man returns, often resents what she feels is his usurpation of her hard earned authority.

WOMEN'S STATUS

A traditional Hindu practice, still performed in some conservative households, is for the wife to wash the feet of the husband at night. In an extremely conservative household the wife will then drink a small amount of this water.

This practice has almost disappeared now, but it does illustrate the traditional position of women in the marriage. Feet are considered the most polluted portion of the body, and it is hard to imagine anything more demeaning than to drink water used to wash another person's feet.

Only marriage confirms a woman as a full member of Hindu society; without it she has little ijjat. Both she and her parents suffer spiritually and in the community if she remains unmarried: she because marriage is so fundamental to a woman's worth, they because they have failed to find her a husband.

In the hill tribes' non-Hindu cultures, the woman has her own identity without her husband. She enjoys more freedom and authority both inside and outside the marriage. Power is shared more openly and evenly, but still the dominant position belongs to the husband.

Hill tribes may not be Hindu, but even there an unmarried woman (or man) suffers loss of face and position in the community. Since marriage is almost universal, those who do not marry are considered strange.

House and Farm Manager

The practical work of managing the household is often left to the highest ranking woman in the family, who decides who does what work and when it gets done. She may ask her husband for his final approval, but she is the manager.

Especially in agricultural matters the wife often knows more than men. Most husbands will listen very carefully to their wife's advice and rely on it when it comes to farming. In the hill tribes power is more evenly shared and more openly shared as well.

A Wife's New Home

When a woman marries, she accompanies her husband back to his home. Until she gets married, her parents' home is her home, her *ghar*. After she marries, her parents' home is no longer her ghar. That term is used to refer to her new home with her husband. Her

Transplanting rice is traditionally done by women on a communal basis with families exchanging labor. Most of the field work is done by women.

parents' home becomes her *maita*, her refuge from the hardships of her new home.

In her new home, the bride finds her status radically and abruptly changed. From the beloved daughter of the household, she often finds she has become little more than a servant.

She arrives in her new home a complete stranger, with no friends or support. Her status is lower than that of any other family member. She will be given the most arduous jobs of the household, with her work continually scrutinized and criticized, particularly by her mother-in-law and sisters-in-law.

In conservative households a daughter-in-law may be expected to *dougnu* (touch her forehead to their feet) her husband and mother-in-law each morning as a greeting. This gesture is a physical indication of her low status in the family.

Her position can only improve if a younger brother marries and brings his wife home. Then the new wife is given the lowest status in the family. A wife's position may also improve when she produces a son.

Escape

To escape the stress of the married household, a wife periodically returns to her parents' home. Holidays such as Tij, Bhai Tika, and Mother's Day allow her to travel and relax in the loving atmosphere of her own home. After giving birth to a baby, it is common for the woman to return and rest at her parents' home for up to one month.

If her position in her married household is unbearable, the woman may stay home until her husband comes or sends someone to fetch her. Or she simply refuses to go back.

DIVORCE

In Hindu belief, marriage is not a matter of free choice. The marriage has been arranged by the parents, but even they are only carrying out what has been predestined in the couple's previous lives. To break such a union is to disobey what the gods have ordained and a most serious offense.

A divorce is a disgrace and profound failure to perform one's sacred duty. Most of the blame and guilt is laid on the woman. A woman contemplating divorce faces being shunned by her own family as well as the community.

The sixth amendment of the 1963 National Code outlines the grounds and process for divorce and the rights of the parties involved. Adultery on the woman's part is grounds for divorce, adultery committed by the man is not.

The laws concerning divorce settlements favor the man on two crucial points:

1. The woman loses all rights to the man's property and assets.

2. The woman gives up all legal rights to her children when they reach the age of five.

There are regulations specifying that the husband must provide alimony for up to five years, but this is difficult to enforce and there is no real force behind it.

The loss of the children hits hard emotionally and economically, since the elderly in Nepal rely on their children for support.

Divorce can also be a lengthy process, taking up to three years. During this time the woman must support herself since alimony is only available (if available) after divorce.

Within the cultures of the hill tribes there are not the same prohibitions and stigmas attached to divorce. Marriage is a free choice, and so is divorce. A woman (or man) is free to marry again after divorce. However, as tribes become more influenced by Hinduism, this is changing and more conservative attitudes are being adopted.

Widows and Widowers

In Nepal's Hindu society widowhood carries severe burdens. Since the woman's value only came through her husband, the death of the husband is the death of the wife. Widows are often shunned as having failed.

Traditionally they wear plain white and are forbidden from wearing any ornaments. Widows are not allowed to attend family ceremonies, to prevent any of their misfortune from cursing anyone else. Remarriage to anyone but the brother of her deceased husband is impossible. The property of the deceased husband often has to be turned over to the sons, whose charity the woman has to rely on.

Strictures on widows are not as severe in the hill tribes and a woman may remarry without fear of breaking social and religious rules. In general she is free to take part in family ceremonies.

The fate of widows is gradually changing, but once again most of the change is occurring in the urban areas. In many rural areas the fate of a widow is still far from pleasant.

Widowers face little change in their social standing. They may remarry without any criticism and, in fact, may even be criticized if they don't do so.

Daughters: Sacred, Expensive Burden, Unpaid Labor

When you observe a Nepali family (of any ethnic group), it often seems that the daughters are little more than unpaid labor. This is especially true in Hindu families.

Hindu religion ingrains the woman's role of sacrifice and duty to the household, first her parents', then her husband's. Parents start instilling these qualities in girls almost as soon as they can walk.

A girl starts working as soon as she can carry a basket or another baby. She takes care of her younger siblings (even if she is only five years old). Sacrificing her education, she joins the other female family members in the fields while her brothers go off to school. Sacrificing her health, she eats after everyone else has, getting the poorest quality and smallest amounts of food.

This does not mean her life is complete drudgery. She laughs and plays with her brothers and sisters just like children everywhere do; but in a country without enough opportunities to go around, girls are most often the ones to be denied access to them.

As a girl becomes older, and the problem of arranging her marriage begins to loom, she becomes in many ways a burden to her family, a source of considerable worry and expense. The burden may be a sacred one, but a burden nonetheless.

Daijo and Tilak

Daijo and *tilak* illustrate that the bride herself is not worth much; it is what she brings with her that gives her value.

Dowry payments (the money, gold, gifts, and other assets a bride brings with her into the marriage, given to her by her family) is not as big a problem in Nepal as it is in India. The Terai, the area closest to India, is where it is most strictly observed and causes the most problems.

A dowry is meant to be a farewell gift to the bride, giving her some assets and wealth of her own within her marriage, like her own private bank account for emergencies. The dowry is often twisted by the groom and his family into the price the bride's family must pay in order to have a husband for their daughter.

In some cases the groom's family will make demands for gold, and appliances like TVs, videos, and refrigerators. Sometimes a motor scooter or land will be demanded. If the girl is older or there are some doubts about her virginity, the demands will be raised.

In addition to the dowry, there may be another demand for tilak, a payment to the groom for consenting to marry the bride. If the bride has some problem that can make it difficult for her to marry, the groom may demand a substantial amount to marry her. Unlike the dowry, which technically remains the bride's – her security in case something happens – the tilak goes straight to the groom's family. The groom is performing a service by marrying the bride; the tilak is his fee.

The Social Ceremonies Reform Act of 1976 puts a limit of Rs 10,000 and one set of gold ornaments as the amount of dowry a girl may bring with her. It also forbids any negotiations between the families on the amount. The payment of tilak is outlawed completely. Another portion of the act even places limits on the number of guests to be invited to the wedding (100 relatives and 50 friends). But these laws are largely ignored.

Boys: A Gift from The Gods

In Hindu households the birth of a son is a cause for celebration, bringing added status to the mother. Here is someone to carry on the family line. Here is the only person capable of conducting the all-important rites which will enable the dead parents to make a quick trip through death and on to their next rebirth.

Given his importance to the parents' immortal lives and to the continuation of the family line, it is small wonder sons are favored over daughters. If there is only enough money or labor available to send one child to school, it will be the son. The sons may eat before their sisters, and if there is not enough milk to go around, the sons get it first.

In social relations within the family it is usually the son who is indulged most, disciplined the least, pampered the most, allowed to have his own way, and generally made to feel he is king of the house. Mothers in particular dote on their sons.

As a son grows into his teens and starts to have his own opinions about how things should be done, he may find himself often at odds with his father. Both are used to exerting authority in their own spheres and, as their worlds begin to intersect more, there may be tension and even conflict between them.

Both son and father resent and resist the new challenges each gives the other, and this may lead to frequent arguments and power struggles within the household. It is not unusual for a teenage son to become fed up with suddenly not getting his way and resolve the situation by running away, at least temporarily, to the Terai, Kathmandu, or India.

A good dose of the reality of 'life out there' is often enough to end the estrangement and bring the son back to the family, but sometimes the separation becomes permanent, with neither side communicating directly, only hearing of each other through third parties or rumor.

In high caste households, as he observes his parents, the son becomes aware of his high social standing not only in the household, but in the community as well. His high standing is reinforced by the various ceremonies that mark his growing up. By the time he reaches his teens (if not earlier), he becomes aware of the power his status as a high caste Hindu grants him and may start using it in his relations with other villagers.

LAWS OF CULTURE VS. LAWS OF NATION

Nepal has been a unified country for about two hundred years. Throughout most of the country's history the main responsibility of the central government was only national security. This included the maintenance of the central government's all-powerful position. To do this it needed money, and to raise this money it collected taxes.

Maintenance of its position and the collection of taxes was the central government's main concern at the local level. The national government had no real policy or programs for the provision of services to the population until the country started to enter the modern world in the mid-1950s. Until then schools, roads, bridges, health services were largely the responsibility of the local communities.

The same was true with law enforcement. Although there was a national criminal code, it was often ignored. Partly this was because of the long distances involved and communication problems, partly because of the natural tolerance of Nepalis for different cultures, and partly because the government did not have the resources to effectively enforce the national code.

Each tribal group was like a nation unto itself, with its own system for handling the civil, moral, and criminal problems that occurred within it. In most cases localities were allowed to solve local problems themselves, without the imposition of national laws.

The same is true even today. Although the police presence is wider, the nearest policeman may still be a day or more away. Small criminal cases are solved locally without even consulting the police, or with the community jointly deciding on their course of action before consulting the police.

BODY LANGUAGE
The Head

The head is the most sacred part of the human body. Children are rarely patted on the head.

The appearance of a person's head sends out signals. A shaved head on an adult man indicates he is in mourning, probably for a parent deceased within the last year. If he is a young teenager he may have just undergone his bratabandha ceremony.

At the back of every Hindu's head will be a small tuft of longer hair that is never cut, even if the skull is shaved. This is called the tupi and is a symbol that the wearer is a Hindu.

One of the most easily recognizable and commonly seen symbols of Nepal is the topi, the brimless cloth cap you see worn by men and boys everywhere. Men of the Himalayan region and some groups in the Terai are the only ones to abstain from wearing topis. A topi is almost a must for a visit to any government office and is a part of the official uniform of Nepal's civil servants.

Married women wear a streak of red powder in the parting of their hair called sindoor. This red streak is a symbol of their married status, and since marriage raises a woman's status, it is worn with pride. Widows do not wear it.

Another symbol of a woman's married status is the *pote*, a string of small glass beads, often with a gold ornament in the center, worn as a necklace. Only married women can wear these.

Tikas

The universal symbol of Hinduism, common to men, women, and children is the tika, a mark or dot placed in the middle of the forehead. A tika may be a small plastic dot, a smeared line of sindoor, or a forehead-wide mixture of yogurt, rice, and sindoor.

The tika is a mark of blessing from the gods. It is also an acknowledgment and representation of the divine within us all. It's an especially important part of the Dasain festival, a symbol of Durga's great victory and power over evil.

In many pictures of Shiva, he is seen with a third eye placed vertically in the middle of his forehead. This third eye represents the all-seeing, all-knowing that comes with complete compliance to the

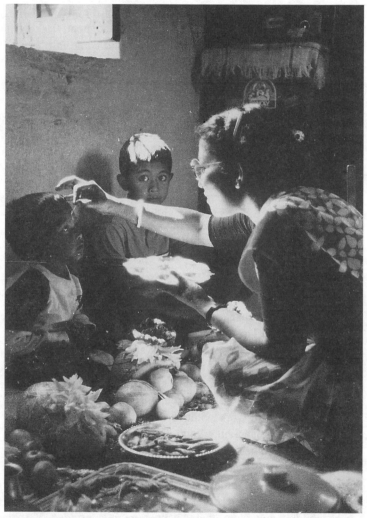

A Nepali woman gives a young boy a tika during the important festival of Bhai Tika. The elaborate piles of fruit and food surrounding the boy are also used in the ceremony.

tenets of the *Vedas*. The tika symbolizes this third eye.

Women have turned the tika into a fashion statement. Packets of plastic tika marks are on sale in the bazaar and come in different sizes, colors and even different designs (stripes, iridescent, metallic). At festivals there is usually a tika shop with women peering into tiny mirrors as they dip small twigs into small vats of different colors mixed with mustard oil, or choose from a pile of plastic dots.

Men don't wear the plastic dots, but receiving a tika, either at home or at a temple on the way to work, is a common part of most men's morning routine.

Receiving a tika is a common part of most ceremonies, an acknowledgment of the divine presence at the occasion and an invocation of divine protection for those receiving it. Receiving a tika on arrival or departure is an indication of the respect and affection of the people involved, bestowing divine protection on the person.

The Body

Most Nepali cultures are quite conservative when it comes to the body and clothing. This goes for both men and women. It may not be very apparent at first, but if you look at how and when the body is displayed, the rules for clothing and the body become clear.

For the first few years a child wears little or no clothing. That's for practical reasons: few families can afford all those diapers, and women have enough work without a pile of dirty diapers. Village Nepal is not very clean either, and it is easier to clean a body than to try and keep clothes clean.

Children start to wear clothing when they are toilet trained. In the hot months of the monsoon, clothing means a pair of ragged shorts that constantly slip to the knees.

As children get older they become more conscious of their bodies and more conservative in their dress. When a girl receives a sari or dress from her parents, or when she reaches puberty, it's time to start observing adult modesty. Boys are very modest, too, even among other men.

Nudity, even if it's casual or accidental, is quite rare, even among adults of the same sex. Dress is very conservative.

Men rarely go shirtless – the shirt may have holes everywhere and be held together by only a few threads, but it is still worn. Women, particularly unmarried ones, are equally conservative. Their tight, bare midriff blouse will fasten in the back. Their shoulders will always be covered.

When a woman marries, things ease a bit: her purity is no longer under constant threat. A mother may sun herself barebacked with her newborn baby, another of the privileges of motherhood. Blouses for mothers and older women fasten down the front.

In old age, standards of dress become more relaxed. Grandpa and grandma sometimes sit topless in the warm sun, letting the sun warm their tired bodies.

Standards of Dress and The Foreigner

Men and women coming to Nepal should dress conservatively. Men should wear at least a T-shirt and a pair of conservative shorts; pants are best. Women should not bare their shoulders, wear haltertops, or short shorts. A long skirt is best and a T-shirt with at least half sleeves.

If you don't meet these community standards, you may not be allowed into temples and other cultural monuments, and you will not be treated with respect.

It is cultural arrogance to assume that the liberalizations that have occurred since the 1960s in Western ideas of proper dress apply automatically to Nepal.

Bathing

There are few homes with indoor plumbing, fewer still with indoor bathing (and even fewer with hot water). Bathing for the majority of

Nepalis takes place at a communal tap or a stream or river.

Public bathing calls for modesty. Men wear a pair of shorts – underwear is OK – at all times while bathing. When it is time to change from wet shorts into dry ones, the man first wraps himself in a *lungi*, the all-purpose 2x1 meter (6x3 ft) cloth that is essential for travel in Nepal. Under the lungi he works off the wet shorts, dries himself and then puts on a pair of dry shorts or underwear. He can then take off the lungi and put on a pair of pants.

Women wear a lungi to bathe, too (and often use two). Wrap yourself up to your armpits in a lungi before removing your top. Wash with the lungi still on. When you've finished bathing, wrap a dry lungi over the wet one before removing it (a long skirt with an elastic waist also works) and then put on your top over the lungi and your bottom half on under the lungi before removing it. Lungis are basically a long skirt and can be worn as one.

Women should note that the characterization of Western women in the media, particularly the videos available in Nepal, are for the most part unflattering, presenting them as constantly looking for a man. Based on what Nepali men have seen, standards of dress that may be acceptable, even normal, at home may be considered provocative in Nepal.

The Feet
The feet are surely the most polluted, profane part of the body. In constant touch with all that is impure in the world, feet and shoes are to be avoided at all costs.

A Nepali will go to great lengths to avoid stepping over any portion of another person, any food or utensils, or a book.

To step over another person would make a statement on the relative social position of the two persons. Nepalis will ask you to move before they will step over you, even if it's only stepping over your feet. They will slide their feet along the floor to avoid lifting their feet higher than any portion of your body.

Nepalis carefully avoid brushing against anyone with their feet. Even accidentally touching someone with your feet should be apologized for immediately.

The form of this apology is to touch your hand to the other person's feet (or at least make the motion) and then touch the hand to your own head as you repeat Vishnu's name. By this gesture you say, "I'm sorry. Your feet are actually higher than my own head." Even good friends will do this if one touches the other with a foot.

Nepalis would not dream of sleeping head to foot, and any statements that it means nothing to you would only leave them feeling very uncomfortable. Sleeping comfort is sometimes sacrificed for cultural comfort.

Never point with your feet, even indirectly, at anyone. This includes pointing at people or images in a temple. If you become tired sitting crosslegged and you want to stretch your legs, either place them so that they aren't pointing at anyone or drape a cloth over them. Stick them under the corner of a mat if neccessary.

Your shoes should also be treated carefully. Never motion at anyone with your shoes or threaten anyone with a shoe, even as a joke. Be careful when taking off your shoes not to place them on top of another person's shoes.

Nepali people usually take off their shoes when entering a home or sitting down at the hearth or on a mat. It may seem inconvenient, but this custom should be followed.

Always remove your shoes before entering a Hindu temple. Look for other shoes to know where to take yours off.

In the Himalayan regions where most people are Buddhists and temperatures are much colder, these constraints may be less strictly followed, but feet and shoes should still be treated with care.

Take your shoes off before entering a *gompa* or monastery, and never point your feet at religious images or texts. Never put your feet or shoes in a home's hearth.

Don't wash your feet in a stream in the vicinity of prayer wheels turned by the stream. If you must use the stream, use it well down-stream of the prayer wheels.

RELATIONSHIPS OUTSIDE THE FAMILY

The caste system can be considered an institutionalization of the divisions that occur naturally in any society. It not only delineates all the various positions and occupations in society, it also assigns each of these divisions a status. Going one step further, it places severe penalties, in this world and the next, on people who break these standards or ignore their own status or that of the people in their life.

Your caste determines your profession, who you can marry, who you can socialize with, who is above you, who is below you, who you can talk to and who you can't.

You proclaim your caste as soon as you say your name. Any attempt to change your name means changing your traditional job, too. It also requires moving far away to a place where no one knows you. All that requires an amount of money few people have in one of the poorest countries in the world. Even if you can escape the strictures of this world, to step outside your caste is to condemn your soul and that of your family to eternal damnation. Few people attempt it.

The Hindu religion also preaches patience. Be content with your lot in this life, perform your duties in this life well, and you will be rewarded with a higher caste in your next life.

Centuries ago the caste system led to a very status-conscious society. Even today very few conversations in Nepal take place between equals. In almost all social encounters, one person's position is superior to the other.

Determining Status

In rural Nepal a person's status is to a large extent determined at birth by two factors: the newborn's sex and caste or ethnic group. A large portion of a person's standing in society is simply presented to them on a platter. The trouble is that the platter may be anything from gold to iron.

In rural society, where the vast majority of people are farmers, the caste of the farmer determines his status in the community. If two people of equal caste meet, then wealth, age, the amount of land they own or any number of factors will be used to determine who outranks whom.

Civil Servants and Falling Status

Traditionally certain jobs confer status: teachers and civil servants always had higher status. There were very few positions available and it was very difficult for anyone but high caste Hindus to get the education and training necessary to obtain such a position.

There are two types of positions: *asthaai* (temporary) and *sthaai* (permanent). To be sthaai is a little like being tenured. It is extremely difficult to be fired, pay is a little better, and a pension is due on retirement. Asthaai people have none of these. When the funding for their position is ended, there is no guarantee another position will be found for them. Of course a person can move from being asthaai to sthaai, but there are never enough permanent positions to go around.

Neither position pays as well as a good job in the private sector, but in the 'old days' the status given to teachers and civil servants compensated for their low pay. The huge amounts of foreign aid coming in helped create a new set of rules. Costs have gone up, but salaries haven't.

The projects create 'temporary' positions that die when the project is finished. There is no job security or pension. A job may last a few months, a few years and then be gone. It may take years to get another job.

People have to make the best of an opportunity. There have always been perks and privileges, rules could be bent for the right people. In a highly hierarchical, autocratic society like Nepal, this is especially true.

There has always been corruption. The huge amounts of money coming in were temptation without adequate caveats. Perks were extended to everything, from private use of project and government vehicles to 'study tours' abroad. Antiquated accounting practices left loopholes project funds could 'disappear' through. Corruption became an open secret, a subject of teashop gossip.

As corruption has grown, the status and esteem of civil servants has sunk. Sadly, some now consider it part of the system, and many see it as a necessity to make ends meet as inflation continues to grow faster than pay.

Sources

Personal relationships are very important to get things done in Nepal, where the volume of work often exceeds the ability of the system to handle it. You can wait three months to get something done, but you only have to meet the right person and it will be done in three days.

People build up networks of relatives, classmates, co-workers they can call on if needed. The ability to contact the key person, to cut through the red tape, is called 'source'.

"*Source chhinna* (I have no source)," you will hear Nepalis say when you ask why they didn't get a job or contract. Whether it is true or not, it's the reason they believe they didn't get a job.

Another sentence you will hear is "*Aphno manchhe chhinna* (I don't have my own person)." Aphno manchhe is someone to lobby for you, a source of information, a friend, relative, or someone who owes you some kind of debt.

The relation between source or aphno manchhe and the person they help is not one-sided. Using source or aphno manchhe runs up debts and obligations to them. Favors and assistance given must be reciprocated when the time comes.

Chamchhas

"He is so-and-so's *chamchha*," you will hear whispered. Chamchha means spoon and is a derogatory term. A chamchha is a spoon feeding someone anything they can: mainly money or material goods, but also information and gossip. A chamchha implies corruption. Chamchhas are different from sources. They usually rely on the patronage of the person they are providing for to keep their job. There is also a regular on-going relationship between the chamchha and the person they're providing for.

Showing Respect

Namaste roughly translates as 'I salute the divine within you'. It is exchanged when two people meet and when they part. A variation used to show more respect is *Namaskar*. Both terms come from Sanskrit.

Namaste is usually accompanied with a gesture. Your hands are joined palm to palm, finger tip to finger tip, in front of your chest, with the fingertips pointing straight up at your chin, like praying. Both Hindus and Buddhists use this gesture.

Like most things in Nepal, this gesture is not as simple as it may first appear. The status of the people involved is a determinant factor. In rural Nepal a high caste Chhetri or Brahmin would barely acknowledge the gesture of a low caste Sarki or Damai, and almost certainly not return it.

A lowly clerk may greet his boss with his joined palms raised to his forehead, bowing forward at the same time. When his boss returns the gesture his hands may barely reach above his stomach, or he may simply raise one hand in a half-wave.

Generally speaking, the higher the joined palms are, the more respect is being given. Sometimes the palms may even be raised above the head. Bowing forward adds respect, too. When the gesture is given to royalty, the person giving the Namaste will be bent double, with the hands above the forehead and eyes downcast.

Namaste and You

As a foreigner who is outside the complex social structure, you need not be as concerned about how high your hands are, whether you should bow, whether to return that Namaste or not. You will be most often treated as an honored guest, particularly if it is perceived you have helped or can help the village, office or ministry. A non-commital, hands-in-the-middle-of-the-chest gesture will see you fine through most situations, and a friendly smile as you do it is a big help.

Forms of Address

People rarely call each other by their name; even parents don't call their children by name. Wives in many parts of the country are very reluctant to name their husband because of superstition: bad spirits may hear and plague him with bad luck.

When people do use names, in most formal and semi-formal situations, the suffix -*ji* will be added to the person's name. Ji is an all-purpose honorific used with both men and women's names. Ram becomes Ram-ji, Manju becomes Manju-ji. Nepalis will also use it with foreign names, such as Dave-ji and Mary-ji. However, good friends call each other by name only.

In many formal situations, a person will be called *hajur* or *yahaa*. These can be translated as respectful ways of saying 'you', but can also be translated as 'your honor' or 'your esteemed self'. It's almost like being addressed as royalty, and you will hear some people respond to this by using *hami* (we), a sort of royal 'we', instead of *ma* (I).

In informal, casual situations where names are not known, people are addressed as if they were a family member, based on what their position relative to the speaker would be. An older man becomes *daai* (older brother), a younger woman is *bahini* (younger sister). An elderly person calls younger men *babu* (used with baby boys) and often calls women *chori* (daughter).

Below is a list of terms used to address family members:
Grandfather – *baaje*
Grandmother – *amaa, hajur amaa*
Father – *bua*
Mother – *amaa*
Older brother – *daai, daaju*
Older sister – *didi*
Younger brother – *bhaai*
Younger sister – *bahini*
Son – *chora*
Daughter – *chori*

Within the family, children are called not by their name, but by their position according to birth: oldest son, third-born daughter, youngest daughter, youngest son. For sons, the eldest is *jetha*, the second *maai*, third *saaila*, and youngest *kaancha*. For daughters, the corresponding terms are *jethi, maaili, saaili,* and *kaanchi*. It is not rare for parents to have a hard time recalling their children's real names after a decade of calling them by their position.

Cousins are referred to as brother or sister. There are dozens of specific terms for each relative in the family: *maamaa* is mother's brother, *kaakaa* is father's brother.

Maamaas are famous in Nepal for lavishing presents and treats on nephews and nieces. Foreigners, who have a reputation for handing out candy on the trail, are sometimes called 'maamaa'. Maamaas are known for carelessly spoiling children with their free handouts and its use is not really complimentary.

Other Signs of Respect
Garlands are a common form of showing respect in Nepal. Strings of marigolds and sweet smelling flowers are draped over the necks of honored guests as they arrive or leave. The person receiving the garland should lean forward as the garland is given and acknowl-

edge it with a Namaste gesture. The Himalayan groups present a *katha* (see below) to departing guests.

Offering a tika, the red powder mark of blessing on the forehead, is another form of showing respect.

It is not uncommon to see a person, after exchanging a greeting with an older person, incline their head toward the older person and for that person to then place a hand (or hands) on the forehead of the first person. A blessing from the older person to the younger, and also from a higher status person to a lower.

Another gesture of respect that can be a little startling and disconcerting when first seen is the dougnu. In this gesture a person bows down and touches their forehead to the feet of another person. This is a sign of great respect.

It is most commonly seen from children to parents. A university student returning home after a long absence would be expected to do so. Usually just showing a willingness to dougnu is enough. The person receiving the dougnu reaches forward and lightly stops the person from completing it.

It can be a sign of great respect and affection when exchanged between parent and child, but it can also be a sign of great abasement and servility when a tenant farmer or day laborer gives it to a local landlord who ignores the gesture.

Himalayan Groups

Himalayan groups also use the Namaste gesture. As an additional sign of respect, particularly when visiting a lama, they will present a katha, a long white scarf, usually made of cotton. When it is presented to a lama, an additional presentation of money and food is usually placed at one end of the katha and loosely covered by it. After the gifts are presented, the katha is draped over the head and shoulders like a scarf. The katha is commonly given as a gesture of respect when a guest leaves.

It is a good idea when traveling into Himalayan areas to carry a few kathas to be used when visiting lamas or other high-placed people in the local community. These can be easily purchased in Kathmandu.

'You'

One of the most obvious ways a person shows their respect for people (or lack of it) is the term used to address them. There are a variety of terms used to address people in both the second and third person, implying whether the person is of higher, lower, or of the same status as the person addressing them.

Different forms of 'you':

• *Hajur, hazur, yaahaa*: the most respectful terms.

- *Tapaii*: respectful, used for people of equal status. This is the most frequently used and an all-purpose term.
- *Timi*: a term of endearment or mild insult. Used between good friends, a husband and wife (usually husband to wife), parents to children. Also used by a boss to his subordinates and from someone of high caste and status to someone of lower caste and status. It is used in arguments.
- *Ta*: the least respectful term, used to address animals or people of low status. It is sometimes used to address children or by a husband to his wife. Used to address someone of very low caste and status or in the heat of a real argument.

Non-native speakers find 'tapaii' fine in most instances. You should address children as 'timi' and avoid using 'ta'. As you gain experience in the language, you may start to vary your usage.

The term *solti* is a term of respect and friendship used between men. Gurungs and Tamangs use it to refer to a cousin (mother's brother's son). In Gurung and Tamang culture, marriage with a solti's sister is very favorable, so calling someone a solti is making him a special cousin.

Welcomes and Goodbyes

At important occasions, five small girls called *Panchakanya* will greet the most honored guests and bid them goodbye when the ceremony is over. The girls must be virgins and are usually pre-pubescent. They present the guests with flower garlands (*maalaas*). The Panchakanya represent five important women in Hinduism:

1. Ahily, the first woman, created by Brahma and wife of the great wiseman Gautam
2. Sita, wife of Ram in the *Ramayana*, famous for her piety and selfless devotion to her husband
3. Draupadi, devoted wife of the five Pandava brothers in the *Mahabharata*, famous for her chastity and piety

4. Tara, wife of the monkey king Bali in the *Ramayana*
5. Mandodari, wife of the villainous demon Ravana in the *Ramayana*, who begged him to return Sita to Ram

The invocation of these five virtuous and pious women is considered to be very auspicious. Their worship was encouraged by Manu, the initial law-giver of Hinduism.

Horns and Water Jugs

Any major guest can expect to be greeted with blowing horns, beating drums, and cheering crowds. With so little excitement in Nepal, it doesn't take much to attract a crowd, and the visit or arrival of a foreigner is probably the biggest event there in quite a while.

Arriving on foot, you may be greeted at some distance from your destination and invited to rest for a moment and offered tea and snacks. It would be impolite to refuse. When you start off again you may be preceded by Damais blowing large horns and beating on drums. Local dignitaries may accompany you, but you will be asked to walk in front. You may already be draped in flower garlands and given a tika.

The trail may have arches of greens, banana tree fronds, for example, with red banners proclaiming '*Swargatam*' (welcome).

At the base of each side of the arch you may see a *gaagro*, the ubiquitous water jug of Nepal. These must be full of water and probably will be covered in flowers as well. To pass between full gaagros is very auspicious. Gaagros will also be placed at the entrance to any building with an honored guest coming or leaving.

At the actual site of the ceremony, the Panchakanya are waiting. The participants in the ceremony may also be given tikas. The ceremony, with speeches by local dignitaries, follows. You may be asked to make a speech. After the ceremony, there may be a 'cultural show' of songs and dances by schoolchildren. There may also be a meal or snacks of some kind.

As the guests leave, they may be garlanded again and receive tikas as a parting benediction. Visitors to the hill tribes may find their head and shoulders coated with red tika powder. This is a gesture of blessing and affection, so expect it after a long stay, where there has been time to build up personal relationships.

The Center of Attention

Remember that no matter how ordinary you feel you are, to the average Nepali you are something very, very special indeed.

Be prepared to be stared at. Staring is not considered rude or discourteous. If you are in public, you are subject to public scrutiny. People (especially children) will want to watch your every move, peer over your shoulder as you read and write, stare at your watch, rub your clothes, touch your skin.

While you are being stared at, don't be surprised if you are discussed as if you were an exhibit in a museum. Some people find this grates on their nerves. If it's any consolation, they're probably wondering how much your shoes cost.

If the people watching you can speak a little English, they may start asking questions. Where are you from? Are you married? Any children? What's your job? Why did you come here? What's your salary? How much does the ticket cost to your country? How long does it take? How much does your watch, radio, camera, etc. cost?

If you can speak even a little Nepali, be prepared to be peppered with questions about yourself and why you are there.

What can you do about all those questions? Be patient, be very patient. It is important not to display anger or irritation. Nepalis don't consider it anything to get upset about: how else will they learn anything about you and foreigners? And they don't know you've been asked the same thing by 20 other people.

The best way to stop questions is to simply go some place else. If you are walking on the trail, make an excuse to stop or go off the trail. Say you need to go to the toilet or something. Tell the person you're a slow walker and you don't want to hold them up anymore.

PRIVACY

Physical privacy is not the accepted right it is in Western cultures. When you are on the trail, you can be observed without reservation.

If you are staying in a Nepali house, you may find your lack of privacy particularly frustrating. People walk in your room, sit down, and watch you.

In Nepal, if you are home, your door is open. Why would you lock your door if you're home? A barred door (like a barred office) is an indication you are doing something you shouldn't be doing.

FRIENDSHIP

One thing you will do in Nepal is make friends. Even if you only stay for a day or two, you'll probably leave with a few addresses of new friends scribbled on paper (with requests for a copy of that photo you took).

A smile and a nod are enough to start a conversation, and Nepalis have made conversation an art. Without newspaper, television, and very limited radio, most of their information comes orally, and a new face is a source of new information.

Friendships and Influence

Foreigners occupy a special position in Nepal. You have come from so far, and at great expense. You have education and are perceived as having more money and more material possessions than most Nepalis can dream of having. You are a person of power and status.

People will see nothing wrong with asking you to help them. A person you regard as your friend asks you to get him the peon's job at the school you teach at, a farmer who has invited you to lunch several times asks you to help get his son into an exclusive school even though the son failed the entrance exam.

You may feel as if you're being used (and you are), but people use their connections like that. People with the best connections often get ahead of people with more merit. Everybody is using connections, and if the person concerned is qualifed, why not put in a good word for him. If you help, that's fine, and if you can't or don't, that's fine too.

GIFT-GIVING

Gift-giving normally takes place within the family. It's common to give a present the first time you see a baby, or if you are invited to some life passage ceremony. Simply hand the gift with your right hand or both hands to the host or whomever you're giving the present to.

Don't expect a big fuss to be made over your present. Chances are it will not be opened in your presence and it will probably not be acknowledged. This is to avoid any embarrassment to either the giver or receiver. If the person is disappointed or doesn't like the gift, they don't want to show it.

Gifts outside the normal gift-giving occasions tend to make people uneasy. They don't know what to do with it or how to treat the gift – why would you give them a gift?

Traditional gifts are food, cloth (or readymade clothing), and money. Food usually means fruits and sweets. Money is always welcome. Traditional gift-giving times are Dasain and Bhai Tika during the Tihar celebration.

It is customary to receive a new set of clothes at Dasain. If you have employees in your household, they will expect you to give them a new set of clothes (in addition to a bonus of one month's salary). For women this usually means a sari and cloth to make the petticoat and blouse. Men usually get a shirt, pants, perhaps a sweater or jacket. Since these new clothes are used to visit family and friends during the Dasain festivities, street clothes, not work uniforms, are more appropriate.

The other major gift-giving occasion is Bhai Tika during the

Tihar celebrations. Brothers present their sisters with clothes and money after receiving a tika from them. This tika guarantees the brothers' prosperity and long life. The gift is a token of the brothers' thanks and of their pledge to support their sisters at all times.

Birthdays

Many people do not know when their birthday is, and celebrations of birthdays are an event only for the tiny urban middle class.

TIME

Bholi-parsi means 'tomorrow or the day after tomorrow' and is heard in answer to the question, 'When will it be done?' People living and working in Nepal hear it often: in shops, stores, offices, everywhere. It is a positive-but-indefinite answer to a question (it may take longer than the day after tomorrow). It expresses sympathy with the person asking or making the request, but is also an indirect indication that the person answering does not place an extremely high priority on it.

Ideas of office time and punctuality are relatively new and ambiguous in a largely agricultural society where most people still measure their day by the position of the sun and the rumbling in their stomach.

Punctuality

Nepalis can be quite punctual where important events in their life are concerned. For a wedding, the exact time of birth of the bride and groom are compared and used to calculate the exact moment that will be most auspicious for their marriage. The fact that in most villages there are few watches, that the watches are almost always worn by men, and that men are usually not present at the moment of birth are ignored.

But even at the wedding ceremony, time is not cut and dry. At a wedding I attended, the watch of the officiating priest was running noticeably slower than most of the guests'. They questioned him several times and finally a large group converged around him pointing at their watches in exasperation and saying the auspicious moment was long gone. The priest simply shook his head and said his time was correct and added blithely, "What's a few minutes, anyway?"

Rural Time

In agricultural areas, which means most of Nepal, the day is commonly divided into blocks. Minutes and hours are largely ignored and meals are the benchmarks for measuring time. Morning is before the morning meal. After the morning meal is sometimes called 'office time'. Then there is afternoon, late afternoon (usually after the closing of the office) and night (before the evening meal). Nepalis tend to go to bed right after the evening meal, so no meetings will take place after that.

People say they'll meet you in the morning, but that can mean anytime between 7 a.m. and 9 a.m. A person who agrees to meet you after the morning meal could show up any time between 9 a.m. and 12 noon.

Official Time

Offices in the private sector often keep a Western style, 5-day 9 to 5 work week. Government offices keep a 6-day 10 to 5 work week (3:00 on Friday) with Saturday off. In the winter months government offices close at 4 p.m.

Many people don't show up in their office until 10:30 or later, and have a way of disappearing in the late afternoon. There is also a tea or tiffin break at about 1 p.m.

In office situations, especially in His Majesty's Government offices, punctuality and the value of time often seem to be determined by the status of the people involved. If the person you are meeting feels he is higher than you, be prepared to be kept waiting or forgotten altogether if someone of higher status than you suddenly appears or calls on the telephone for a quick meeting.

Walking Time

When you are walking on the trail and ask someone how far it is to your destination, there are a number of possible ways he'll give you an answer. The least likely will be in kilometers. Your answer may come back as so much time, but take this with a grain of salt. Does he have a watch? Time varies tremendously from a Nepali carrying nothing to a porter carrying 40 kilograms. A Nepali usually knows how long it takes him, and because you are a foreigner, figures it will take you twice as long.

A more reliable measure is the number of *kosh* to your destination. A kosh is a measurement based on how far a fully loaded porter can walk in a certain amount of time. The government has standardized the kosh to be a distance of two miles (3.2 kilometers) for its accounting and travel allowance measurements, but local people still measure it as distance over time.

Since you aren't carrying 40 kilos as you walk, you can cover a kosh in considerably less time than a porter. Kosh take into account the uphills and downhills of the trail, and you'll be surprised at the regularity you cover the distance with, once you develop a walking rhythm.

Fully loaded porters walk about eight kosh in a day, average walkers cover about 11. Young civil servants walk phenomenal distances in a day. The reason is government travel allowances are based on the number of kosh. If you walk 33 kosh in two days instead of three, you save one day's expenses and get the same amount of money.

In the far west there is an even more original measurement. Distances are often measured by *hooka*, the ubiquitous pipe smoked by men in the west. It may be three hookas to your destination, which means the average man has the urge to smoke three times between here and there. A hooka does not seem to be as far as a kosh.

Calendars

There are five calendars in use in Nepal. The official one is the Vikram Sambat calendar, named after the North Indian king who is credited with devising it. Day 1 of the Vikram Sambat calendar was February 23, 57 B.C. The year 1991 is 2048 V.S. It is the most commonly used one in government offices and outside Kathmandu.

The Vikram Sambat calendar is a lunar one. There are 12 months varying from 29 to 32 days in length. A month's length may vary from year to year. These adjustments must be made each year because of the lunar basis of the calendar. The next year's calendar is not known or published until relatively late in the present year. Because of the yearly adjustments and changes, comparative dates with the Gregorian calendar dates change from year to year. The new year starts with Baisaakh (mid-April).

The Gregorian calendar is in common use in business and in development organization offices in Kathmandu, but one with both V.S. and Gregorian calendars on it is extremely useful.

Other calendars in use in Nepal are the Newari calendar, the Sakya Era calendar, and the Tibetan calendar.

The Nepali government's fiscal and budgetary years start in Saaun (mid-July). Government funding for projects is frozen one month prior to that in Asaar (mid-June) and this should be taken into account for project planning. Release of the new fiscal year's funds at the district level can also be a very slow process.

Below is the Vikram Sambat calendar :

Month	*Starts in*
Baisaakh	mid-April
Jeth	mid-May
Asaar	mid-June
Saaun	mid-July
Bhadau	mid-August
Asoj	mid-September

Kaartik	mid-October
Mangsir	mid-November
Pus	mid-December
Maagh	mid-January
Phaagun	mid-February
Chait	mid-March

FESTIVALS

On any given day it's probably safe to say there's a festival some-place in Nepal.

Although there are some secular holidays, almost all the major

A demon rushes through the streets of Bhaktapur pursued by a horde of children. Everyday in Nepal there is a festival somewhere. Dancing and the constant battle between gods and demons are popular themes, teaching as they entertain.

holidays and festivals are based around some religious celebration. The differences between Hindus and Buddhists mean that what is a big festival for one group can be just another day to the other group.

Some festivals are nationwide, like Bhai Tika, while others are specific to a certain area. For example Indra Jatra, the grandest festival of the Kathmandu Valley, is only celebrated there. Some festivals also celebrate mankind and human life. Bhai Tika, for example, honors the bonds between brother and sister and cele-brates the individual.

Mela

Local festivals are called *melas* and they are like a small town fair. They are usually held during the same phase of the moon in the

A group of hill tribe women on their way to a 'mela'. The large woven baskets they carry on their backs are called 'dokos', supported by a head strap called a 'namlo'. The woman in the center carries an umbrella, another essential for travel in the hills.

154

same month each year. They're held at a local landmark – a big *chautaraa* (resting place) or a *dobhan* (the confluence of two rivers). They often last only one night, taking place under the full moon, for example.

There may be a religious connection. The mela at Tribeni ghat in the Terai is Nepal's largest. On the morning of the full moon of February, over 100,000 people gather on the banks of the river, where it is believed Sita, the wife of Ram, has returned for a bath.

At Tribeni there are circuses, plays, magicians, shops, games, videos, food, and drink; all for this one night. Melas in the hills, with no roads or electricity, have simpler pleasures but are just as anticipated as a trip to Disneyland. Crowds walk for days to spend a day eating, drinking, shopping, gossiping, gambling, spouse-hunting, or just watching everybody else. Groups of young men and young women square off for singing competitions, winners judged more on the wit of their verses than their singing ability.

A Festival Calendar

The dates for festivals are determined using Nepal's lunar calendar and the dates change annually on the Gregorian calendar:

December-January	Seto Machhendranath
February-March	Shiva Raatri (Lord Shiva's Night)
March-April	Baleju Jatra
	Ghora Jatra
April-May	Biskhet Jatra
	Mother's Day
	Raato Machhendranath
	Buddha Jayanti (Buddha's Birthday)
May-June	Mani Rimdu
June-July	Tribhuvan Jayanti
July-August	Naga Panchami (Day of the Snakes)
	Janai Purnima (The Sacred Thread)

August-September	Gai Jatra
	Krishna Jayanti (Krishna's Birth)
	Father's Day
	Tij (Women's Festival)
September-October	Indra Jatra
	Dasain
October-November	Tihar
November-December	Sita Bibha Panchami
	Bala Chaturdasi

Dasain

Dasain is the most important festival of the year. Nepalis will do anything they can to be home for it. All workers receive a bonus, usually one month's pay. Special foods are prepared and everyone receives a present of a new set of clothes. All offices and stores close for most of this 11-day celebration.

Dasain commemorates the victory of good over evil, the goddess Durga destroying the demon Mahisasura who terrorized the earth in the form of a huge water buffalo.

On the first day a small container of dirt is planted with barley seeds. On the ninth day the household sacrifices an animal (fowl, goat, or even a water buffalo). The blood is dripped over vehicles, everything from bicycles to jet planes, to insure Durga's protection for the coming year. The sacrifices are followed by a big feast.

The 10th day celebrates the actual victory of Durga over the demon. Everyone puts on new clothes and visits relatives and friends to exchange greetings and tikas on this day of joy.

On the 11th day the barley, which has grown into bright green sprouts, is distributed by the head of the house and worn on the head as a sign of blessing.

Tihar

Dasain may be as important as Christmas, but Tihar, which follows

Dasain by about a month, has the feeling of Christmas. There are gifts, decorated houses lit at night, special foods, and even a special nocturnal visitor distributing 'presents': Laxmi, goddess of wealth and good fortune, honored during Laxmi Puja.

Five creatures are worshiped during Tihar. On the first day housewives leave food out for crows. Dogs may be kicked and stoned the rest of the year, but on the second day of Tihar they're given flower necklaces, tikas, and fed a banquet. Cows, symbols of Laxmi, are bathed and garlanded on the third day, bullocks on the fourth, and people worship each other and themselves on the last.

At midnight of the third day, Laxmi, riding her owl, visits deserving houses. Homes are cleaned, and tinsel and colored lights or oil lamps are placed everywhere. A path is painted with a mix of red soil and cow manure from outside the door inside to the place where the home's valuables wait for the goddess's blessing. Beside the valuables are a burning lamp, and flowers and food for Laxmi.

Excited children set off fireworks as night settles and the decorative lights are lit.

Women of the neighborhood go singing from house to house and are rewarded with money and food. Men's turn comes the next night (if you have servants, they may come to entertain you).

On the fourth day Newars celebrate their New Year's Day and everyone continues the celebration of Laxmi's visit. The fifth day is most important. All over Nepal brothers travel to their sisters' homes to receive Bhai Tika (brother blessing). This blessing is so important that, if a boy doesn't have a sister, a relative will act as a sister. In return for the blessing, the sister receives gifts of cloth and money.

Tij

Tij is Nepal's only festival for women, but it is only for Hindu women, although some hill tribe women also celebrate it. Even though it means fasting for at least a day, these women look forward to the three days of Tij, their only break from household duties. On the first day, women of the house eat as grand a feast as possible, because the second day is a total fast.

The fast replicates one done by Parbati as she prayed Shiva would marry her. Shiva did marry her, and in return Parbati promised anyone who fasted as she had a good marriage and many children.

All day groups of women gather by rivers and streams. After bathing they dress in their best clothes, usually a bright red sari, and worship Shiva. Friends and neighbors gather to sing and dance long into the night. On the morning of the third day each woman makes an offering of food to her husband and can break her fast. A ritual bath ends the festival.

Shiva Raatri

This is perhaps the most exotic festival of the Kathmandu Valley. Each February during Shiva Raatri, tens of thousands of people bathe in the Bagmati River at the point where it flows by Pashupathi Temple. People come from all over India and Nepal on the 14th day of the waning moon, the anniversary of a night Shiva spent here in meditation.

Shiva is said to love the spot so much he returns on the same night each year to meditate again. By spending the night in meditation and bathing at dawn, the pilgrims gain great favor with him.

The woods near the temple become a huge campground, lit with the fires of thousands of pilgrims chanting and trying to keep warm. At the first light of dawn people start bathing in the icy river, then stand in line for hours to pour a little of the river water over a stone lingam representing Shiva inside the Pashupathi Temple.

Raato Machhendranath

Each year the great god Raato (red) Machhendra is taken from his temple, placed in a wagon topped by a 12 m (40 ft) spire of pine covered bamboo, and pulled through the narrow streets of Patan. Stops are made in each neighborhood to give everyone a chance to worship. Raato Machhendra is believed to control the monsoon rains so it is vital to keep him happy.

The wagon rams houses, the spire threatens to fall over, wheels get stuck in gutters. Every neighborhood takes a turn pulling the wagon.

The climax comes in an open field where the king comes to display a sacred vest given ages ago by the Serpent King to Raato Machhendra for safekeeping. The exhibition of the vest guarantees plenty of rain for the coming rice crop. Tens of thousands of on-lookers cheer as the king holds the vest high for all to see.

Holi

The festival of Holi is celebrated in the hills and Kathmandu, but to really see it right you have to travel to the Terai. It celebrates the triumph of Krishna over a demoness named Holika. The celebration of her destruction evolved into the present practice of *rang khelne* (play with color), throwing red powder and balloons filled with dye at people.

Supposedly only people who want to play are legal targets, but foreigners often seem to be fair game no matter what their inclination is. In recent years harassment of young women, called 'Eve Teasing' in India, has grown more popular. The main day is on the full moon, Holi Purnima, when crowds of men covered head to foot in red powder dance and sing in the streets.

Indra Jatra

Indra, the god of rain, came to the valley to get some beautiful flowers for his mother, riding his elephant and disguised as a mortal. The local people caught and tied him in heavy ropes like a common thief. Indra's mother came for him, and the people released him as soon as she told them who he was.

In return, she granted them two boons. She took to heaven everyone who died that year and she gave the valley the moist, foggy winter mornings that help the crops even today.

Indra Jatra is also used to worship the terrible god Bhairab, the destroyer. Every neighborhood puts a mask of this terrifying deity on display and worships him. The two most famous ones are the Seto (white) Bhairab at Hanuman Dhoka and the Akash (sky) Bhairab at Indrachowk.

From Seto Bhairab's mouth a bamboo pipe spouts rice beer for three nights. Young men wrestle to take a drink – without touching the pipe with hands or mouth. Somewhere in the flow is a small fish that guarantees prosperity in the next year if it is drunk.

Beautifully costumed and masked dancers wander around Kathmandu re-enacting the victory of Indra over a group of demons. Indra's elephant, two men in a papier-mâché disguise, careens through the small alleys knocking over people in its search for its master.

For three nights the Kumari, the living goddess, is drawn through the streets. On the second night, as thousands wait, she gives a tika to the king. Steering the Kumari's huge wagon is almost impossible. Power poles are bent, roofs knocked off, legs broken.

Buddhist Holidays

Losar, or New Year's Day, is the major festival of Himalayan peoples. Celebrated over several days usually in mid-February, it's a time for dressing up in the best clothes, visiting family and friends, and lots of eating and drinking.

Boudhanath is the best place to watch it in the Kathmandu Valley. With colorful processions and big crowds stringing prayer flags, a photo of the Dalai Lama, the spiritual leader of Tibetan Buddhists, is carried through the crowd. At the exact moment determined by astrologers, everyone hurls handfuls of tsampa flour into the air (and then at each other). Groups of people form long lines, arms over each others' shoulders, and dance in a slow shuffle.

Buddha Jayanti

On the full moon of April or early May, the birth of the Buddha is celebrated throughout Nepal's Buddhist community. People make trips to a monastery, where lamas hold special services, and there are feasts and visiting of friends and relatives. In Kathmandu, Swayambhu is the center of the celebrations, with thousands climbing the 300 steep stairs to the top to worship at the many shrines around the stupa.

Festivals of The Family and Home

Mother's Day is called *aamaa-ko mukh herne din* (See Mother's Face Day). All the children, even those who have married and moved away (usually daughters), return home. They present sweets, fruits, and other gifts to their mother and bend down to touch their forehead to her feet as a sign of their respect. Mother places her hand on their forehead as a sign of blessing.

Father's Day, *buaa-ko mukh herne din*, is celebrated in much the same way.

For Raksha Bandhan, sisters tie decorated silk threads around their brothers' right wrist and give a tika as signs of sisterly affection and devotion. In return brothers give presents and promise to look after them all their life.

It is not uncommon for Nepali houses, usually only clay brick or mud and rock, to collapse in the heavy monsoon rains. Nepalis blame this on the anger of the snake gods living in the ground beneath the house. To keep the snake gods happy, on Naga Panchami, every family fixes a picture of the Serpent King and his retainers above the home's main door. A bright red tika is given to the Serpent King's forehead, the snakes are prayed to and offerings of milk, honey, curd, and rice are placed outside.

Chapter Six

FOOD AND FOOD CUSTOMS

With so many groups of people living in such different environments and with the difficulties of transporting and storing food, diet changes radically from one geographic zone to another. Food supplies are often very scarce and large areas of the country experience food shortages.

A common greeting on the trails of Nepal is "*Khaanaa khaiyo*? (Have you eaten?)" The fact this has to be asked is an indication of the difficulties of getting this most basic of necessities in one of the poorest countries in the world.

The Terai produces surpluses of rice, wheat, and other crops, but large areas of the rest of the country are deficit areas. To feed the people there, food must be brought in. Nepal's almost non-existent road system means most of the grain and other foodstuffs must be brought in on the back of a pack animal or, more often, a porter.

Large areas of Nepal have this problem, particularly in the central and western regions of the country. Food shortages are cyclical, following the agricultural year, and are most critical in the hot, dry months before the monsoon and the first month or so of the monsoon. Areas without irrigation – most of the country – are the worst affected.

The food shortages lead to malnutrition and a lowering of strength and disease resistance, just at the time when diarrhea and infectious diseases are most dangerous. Infant mortality rates go up markedly during this period.

People buy their food from one of the local large landowners, or from a government food depot that can be days away. With 40% of

A hill family cooks their meal while their sheep graze behind them. Families spend weeks and months from one pasture to another. The jugs on the ground were hollowed from wood.

163

families living below the poverty line, many have to borrow money from the rich to buy food. The debt can be paid off with money, grain, or exchanged labor. Interest rates are normally 10–15% and the value of the grain or the labor given is decided by the person who has loaned the money.

The government sells grain through government food depots. There may be food rationing depending on the local situation and it may take more than a day's walk to reach the depot, with no guarantee there will even be anything there to buy.

Much of the food sold by the government is food aid, donated by foreign governments. It's strange to hear people who have never even been to Kathmandu commenting on the various merits of Thai and Italian rice. *Umaleko chamal* (parboiled rice) is often sold at these depots. Making it taste good is a talent.

THE NEPALI DIET

The 'national meal' of Nepal is dal-bhaat-tarkaari (lentil soup, rice, and curried vegetables). Rice is the food of choice; it is so important to the Nepali psyche that the word for cooked rice, 'bhaat', is freely interchanged with the word for food, 'khaanaa'.

Meat is not a daily feature of Nepali meals. There is no way to refrigerate the meat, so usually slaughter of an animal entails a co-operative effort among households in the village. Meat is usually available on special occasions and during festivals. In urban areas where there may be a butcher shop, it is more readily available and may be a more regular part of the diet.

Rice and Reality

Many types of rice are available in Nepal. Local varieties differ in smell, flavor, and texture. Pokhareli masino, noted for its flavor, and Basmati, known for its delicious fragrance, are two well-known and more expensive favorites. Far western Nepal has been famous for

Bullocks prepare a field for rice planting. Although it is a rare commodity, rice is the favorite food of Nepalis.

centuries for its red rice. Actually pink when cooked, it was once the rice of the kings of the western Khas kingdom. In Kathmandu it is possible to get brown rice, but Nepalis consider brown rice a step down, lower in status than polished white rice.

The realities of farming in Nepal put rice out of reach for daily consumption by much of Nepal's population. Eating rice daily confers status and is only possible for the rich in hill societies. The majority of people eat dhedo.

Most people would be reluctant to confess that they eat dhedo. They would lose face to say that they eat something so lowly.

Dhedo

If you looked in the average rural Nepali household in the evening, you would find the family eating a meal of dhedo (pronounced 'dare-dough'). Dhedo is flour mixed in boiling water until it forms a thick, dough-like paste that can be eaten with the fingers.

Dhedo is usually a mix of different flours. There is a hierarchy to most things in Nepal, including flour. Wheat followed by corn are the preferred flours for use, with *kodo* (millet) ranking last on most people's list. But it is the most common type of dhedo found. Typically several grains are mixed together with millet forming the greatest portion.

When there is no question of compromising their social position, many people will tell you they like dhedo, and some will even admit they've acquired a taste for kodo.

It's eaten like rice: a small lump is taken in the right hand, dipped in the dal, vegetables, milk, or whatever else is available, and popped in the mouth.

Rotis and Chapatis

A thick pancake-like bread called *roti* is also eaten throughout the country, mainly in the Middle Hills and the Himalayas. No yeast is added to the mixture of flour and water. The dough is rolled or slapped into a thick pancake and roasted dry or sometimes fried with oil on an iron or steel griddle placed over the fire.

To eat a roti, break off a piece and, holding it in your right hand, dip it in the dal or use it to pinch some vegetables and eat.

In the Terai, *chapatis* are a main staple. Chapatis are also a type of bread, mainly from wheat flour. No yeast is used, just flour, a little salt, and water. A piece of the dough is rolled into a thin round and dry-roasted on a handle-less flat iron. Sometimes the bread is fried. When the bread is deep-fried, it is called a *puri*.

Milk

Milk, coming from sacred cows, is as important to Nepalis for its religious symbolism as for its health and nutritional value. Milk is the favorite food of Krishna, a cowherd himself and one of the most popular Hindu gods. It is sometimes poured over a Shiva lingam during puja and used in other religious sevices, too. Drinking milk is almost an act of worship in itself.

Dudh (milk) is almost always drunk hot, after it has been boiled. Since water is usually added to milk, it is a good idea to make sure it is boiled (also to protect from tuberculosis). It is often poured over rice at the end of a meal: a sort of not-so-sweet dessert.

Dahi (yogurt) is also common. It is poured over rice, mixed with the vegetables or dal and eaten as a regular part of the meal. It is also eaten thick with sugar or salt. Scrape the film off the top of the yogurt before eating it. *Lassi* is a drink made by thinning yogurt with water, and flavoring with sugar or salt.

The Terai, especially the Janakpur and Nepalgunj areas, is famous for its yogurt and milk products. In Kathmandu, Bhaktapur's dahi is famous. Newars have *juju*, a sweet dahi with extra fat content and spiced with cardamom and coconut. It's delicious.

Makkhan (butter) is used in the Himalayan areas, but in other areas it is clarified to preserve it longer. This clarified butter is called ghyu. Ghyu is expensive. It is used to flavor frying vegetables, but most often melted ghyu is poured over the rice to give it a delicious, very rich, buttery-but-different flavor.

Mahi (buttermilk, pronounced 'moi') is mixed with water and should be drunk with caution – the water may give you stomach problems long after the delicious taste of the mahi is gone.

Milk is also used to make Nepali sweets, many of which come by way of India. *Kher* is a rice pudding made with milk. Other sweets like *barfi* and *peda* are basically milk boiled down to a thick paste with sugar and spices added.

Milk products are also taken for their medicinal properties. Dahi in particular is used to cool the body, help digestion (including the burning of chilli peppers) and to cure diarrhea.

EATING

Hinduism teaches that all our actions have a religious significance, and eating is no exception. What you eat and who you eat it with can have a profound effect on the Dharma (merit) or the *pap* (sin) you earn during your life. The wrong foods, eaten with the wrong people, can have a disastrous effect on your immortal existence.

Buddhism forbids the taking of life, but it does not forbid the eating of meat or fish. The Buddha is believed to have said it is acceptable to eat meat if you have no knowledge the killing was done specifically for you. Since most butchering is done on a community-wide basis by an outsider, people feel they are within the Buddha's guideline.

Beef

The most well-known prohibition of the Hindu religion is that on eating beef. The cow, the former symbol of wealth in a nomadic pastoral society, has been elevated over the centuries to our sacred earth mother. Who could think of eating their own mother?

The same taboos do not apply to the Buddhist groups of the Middle Hills and high Himalayas. In the Middle Hills, where Hindu and Buddhist cultures co-exist so closely, it would be difficult to consume beef without causing a major disturbance in the community. In the Himalayan regions, though, a cow or bullock may 'slip' from the trail, an 'accidental' death that allows the 'finders' of the dead animal to eat it.

Foreigners will often be asked if they eat beef. Nepalis know they do, but they like to hear it 'from the horse's mouth'. One point many Westerners stress is that their beef cattle is generally different from their milk cows. Some Nepalis are satisfied by this; others look at you as if to say, "You think I'm that gullible?"

DIETARY RESTRICTIONS

There are three types of dietary restrictions: those mandated by caste or ethnic group, those mandated by circumstances, and those mandated by superstition.

By Caste

The restrictions on beef have been discussed above. In addition, Brahmins will also not eat the meat of water buffaloes, chickens, or ducks. Chhetris will not eat water buffalo meat. Brahmins and Chhetris are forbidden by caste from drinking liquor. A strict Brahmin will also not eat mushrooms, onion, leeks, tomatoes, or eggs.

Buddhist Newars may not eat chicken, but will eat duck. Tamangs do not allow uncooked garlic, nettles, or buffalo meat inside their house. They have no problem eating it inside their homes, only the food preparation must be done outside. Some Himalayan people may not eat leeks or allow them inside their *gumbas*.

While pork is only formally prohibited to Moslems, it is not a big favorite with any group in Nepal.

By Circumstance

In Hindu households, after the death of the father, the sons must fast and abstain from eating salt, oil, lentils, and meat for a period of 13 days. These restrictions are observed periodically afterward.

On the death of a mother, the children will stop drinking milk for a year; on the death of the father, yogurt is not eaten for a year.

A Brahmin will not eat rice if it has been prepared by someone of a lower position than himself. The trouble is not the rice so much as the water used to cook it. If a lower caste person handles the water, it is polluted, and the rice becomes polluted, too. This restriction only applies to rice cooked in water; rice cooked in milk, for example, does not present a problem.

Once a week or once a month women may abstain from eating certain foods for a day. It may be a total fast, or, more commonly, a woman will not eat any food with salt. This fasting is a spiritual and physical cleansing of the body and mind of impurities. Fasting may take place for certain pujas and a fast is an integral part of the women's festival of Tij.

Food which has become jutho cannot be eaten (see *Jutho*).

By Superstition

Vegetables must be cooked with at least a small amount of oil. Vegetables cooked only in water should be avoided.

A red (chilli) pepper should not be dropped into someone's hand while they eat. The giver and receiver may fall into a quarrel. Only drop the pepper on the side of the plate.

Among Himalayan people, if the spatula being used to stir the dhedo snaps, the woman stirring it can't eat from that pot.

Don't have fish and milk or meat and milk at the same time.

MEALS

In most areas of Nepal people eat twice a day. The first meal is in the morning, sometime between 8 and 10, and the second in the evening, between 6 and 8. Evening meals in urban areas tend to be later. Eating the evening meal is usually the last activity of the day: after eating it's time for bed. When being entertained in a Nepali home, the meal will be served late and guests will start leaving for home soon after they have finished eating.

In addition to the two large meals, it is common to eat a light mid-afternoon snack. This is called *kaaja* or sometimes by the English word 'tiffin'.

Where it is available, people start the morning with a glass of sweet milk tea. If there is no sugar, black tea with salt may be drunk. Where tea is not available, raksi may be warmed and drunk. In the Himalayan region tea flavored with salt and butter is drunk.

A mother serves her children the morning meal. She uses a long handled 'dardnu' to place rice on the plates. The 'dal' and 'tarkaari' for the meal are on top of the stove, called a 'chulo'. As in most Nepali homes, this one has no chimney.

Etiquette while Eating

Before eating it is expected you will want to wash your hands, even if the cleansing is more ritual than physical. Carry a hankie to wipe your hands dry before you start, for your own health.

Meals are usually eaten sitting crosslegged on a *gundri* (a woven mat about 1x2 m or 3x6 ft). Take off your shoes before you sit down. When taking your place it is preferable to walk behind the people who are already seated. Never touch anyone with your feet (see *Body Language*) and never step over food, plates, or a person.

A plate with portions of bhaat (rice) and tarkaari (curried vege-

171

tables) is placed in front of you. The dal may be poured directly over the rice or given in a separate cup. In one corner of the plate will probably be some *achhar* (pickle). It may be sweet, sour, bitter, or spicy. Sometimes a good achhar and tasty rice is a meal in itself.

Meat comes on the rice or separately. Bones go back on the plate or the floor next to it. If there is ghyu, this may be offered, pouring it over the rice after it has been melted. Ghyu is delicious, but it is very heavy and a little goes a long way.

If there is too much rice, ask for some of it to be taken off before you start eating. Once you start, the food on the plate becomes jutho and any leftovers are fed to the dogs. Don't mind the protests of your hosts. It's easy (and flattering to them) to ask for more later. If you leave rice on your plate your hosts may feel let down, that the food wasn't tasty.

A meal is mainly judged by its rice. You can ask for tarkaari three times and say how great it is, but that won't mean as much to your hosts as asking for even just one more spoon of rice.

Use only your right hand to eat. You can drink from a glass using your left hand. Mix a little of the rice and dal together, add a bit of vegetable. Use you fingertips like a spoon and your thumb to push the food into your mouth. As you eat you will be asked if there is anything you need. You will make your hosts very happy by asking for more rice.

If there is anything you want, just ask. The more you eat, the happier your hosts are. If there are bones from the meat you are eating, simply place them on the ground beside your plate.

If your hosts want to give you more food, but you're full, hold your right hand over the plate and say, "*Pugiyo* (enough)." Keep your hand directly over your plate; if you move your hand out of the way a little, it's a signal you're only being polite and that in reality you want some more. If you move your hand out of the way, your host will plop some more rice on the plate even if you are still protesting verbally.

172

Water may be placed in a glass or in a communal brass pitcher. If the water is in a glass, drink normally. When you refill your glass, be careful not to let your glass touch the refilling pitcher. If the water is in a communal pitcher, do not place your lips on the pitcher as you pour the water into your mouth. Be sure you only drink what you have seen boiling or what you have seen purified (or purified yourself).

Proper etiquette is that no one gets up until everyone eating has finished. Since most foreigners eat slowly, there could be a line of people waiting for you. If you notice people are starting to finish, invite them to get up and leave. If you are the first to finish and the other people eating invite you to get up, say *"Bistaari khaanus* (Please eat slowly)" as you get up.

Step outside the house to wash your dirty hand. Since you are a guest, someone may offer to hold the pitcher and pour water over your hands while you wash. If you want to do this yourself, take the pitcher with your left hand.

You will notice that Nepalis vigorously wash their mouths after eating; swirling water in their mouth and spitting, coughing up stuff from deep in their throat and chest. Nepalis feel foreigners are more than a little strange because they don't.

Use only treated water to rinse your mouth and brush your teeth.

JUTHO

In Hindu culture, food and utensils used in the preparation of food must be ritually as well as physically clean. If something is clean it is *saphaa*; if it is ritually clean it is *chokho*.

The only way food or a utensil can become chokho is to wash it in water. No soap is necessary: the water itself is the cleansing agent, purifying simply by its touch.

Eating off a dry plate may be clean from a hygienic point of view, but it is unclean from a religious point of view. That is why plates are rinsed with water before they are used.

Jutho is the state of ritual contamination or pollution. To be jutho is to be unfit to eat or to place food in, like the grossest sewage off a dirty floor.

Food or utensils become contaminated when touched by any of the body's excretions (this usually means saliva) or touched by someone who is contaminated by definition – a low caste person – or touched by an impure part of the body such as the left hand or the feet (or shoes).

Take your first bite of food, touching your fingers on your mouth, then touch your rice again. Everything on your plate is now jutho. You must eat it or it is fed to the dogs. If you pick up an extra piece of meat from your plate and drop on your neighbor's plate, his plate is now jutho and he cannot eat from it.

A wife may eat the food off her husband's plate. That does not mean the food is not jutho, it's more of a comment on her status in the family.

If you touch your lips to a water pitcher, the remaining water in the pitcher is jutho. It must be thrown out, rinsed with water, and filled again before it can be used by someone else.

In a teashop, if a low caste person drinks from a glass or uses a plate, they must wash it themselves and set it to dry. Then someone else will wash it, sometimes purifying it with fire as well as water, before it can be used again.

The concept of jutho is strictly observed by Hindus and, to a lesser extent, by the hill tribes. In the Himalayan areas people hardly observe it at all.

THE HEARTH

In caste Hindu households, the area used to prepare and cook food is off limits to all but the woman who is cooking and men who wear the janai. There may be a railing separating it from the rest of the room, or the kitchen may be raised on a small platform, or *litnu* (mud mixed with cow dung used to coat floors of rural homes) may be used to make the floor a different color. The *chulo* (the mud cooking stove) will be set in a corner of this area.

It is important to respect the sanctity of the kitchen area of Brahmin homes. If a foreigner enters it, it becomes jutho and can only be cleansed by an elaborate puja, costing the household time and money.

Only people who wear the janai and the woman who cooks the meal can eat in the kitchen. Others sit around the perimeter outside the area. Food is dropped from the kitchen area into the plates (the reason for the long handles on spoons and ladles becomes apparent). If the utensil happens to touch anything outside the kitchen area, it becomes jutho and cannot be used until it has been washed again.

In strict Brahmin households the men of the family will take off their clothes and wrap themselves in a white cotton dhoti before entering the kitchen.

Gather Round

In most hill tribes and Himalayan homes, the main room of each home also contains a hearth, a rectangular pit usually 2x1 m (6x3 ft), filled with ash. One side of the hearth butts into a wall, the other three sides are available to sit around. Inside the hearth sits an iron ring on three iron legs that is used as a stand to place cooking pots above the fire.

Guests are welcome to sit around this hearth, and it is the center of the household's life. In the higher altitudes entire winter days may be spent around the hearth and its warming fire. People come in, plop down, get up, and walk out again. Meals are prepared next to the hearth, perhaps right next to you, with not a thought of pollution or jutho.

The greatest place of honor, sort of like 'Dad's chair', is usually at the head of the hearth near the wall. Don't sit here unless the spot is offered to you. Watch what other people are doing to see whether you should take your shoes off.

Even though the hearth is the center of household socializing in the hills and the Himalayas, it also has religious significance in some of the other cultures (the Sherpas consider it sacred, for example). Don't throw your trash in, or your cigerettes, either.

Newars are different from their neighbors because they place their kitchen on the top floor of their house. In town areas this can mean the kitchen is three or more stories up. That's a long way up to carry a 10–15 liter (2.6–3.9 gallon) jug of water on your hip. The kitchen often opens onto a rooftop terrace. Newars have no objection to people being in their kitchen.

Chapter Seven

DEALING WITH NEPALIS

The per capita income in Nepal is about US$180 per year. Compare that with the price of your air ticket. Even if you're only on a short vacation, you probably have more material possesions with you than the average Nepali does in a lifetime, and you probably have more travelers' checks and money than the average Nepali will see in a decade.

A group of six to eight tourists dining at one of Kathmandu's top restaurants may spend more money on their meal than the monthly salary of the waiter who brings it to them. Tourists are charged double or more the price that Nepalis usually pay and they still think it's cheap.

Small wonder that the average tourist is viewed as being a millionaire. In a small survey taken in the Annapurna trekking area, about 20% of the Nepalis thought the tourists didn't have to work for their money, they were just rich naturally and that everyone in their country was the same.

THE EXPATRIATE

Nepal has a good sized expatriate community, almost all of whom are involved in development work. The government periodically tries to cut back on the number of development workers, particularly experts, who are allowed in to work as advisers on development projects. Within the development communities there are two main groups: the volunteers and the experts.

The Volunteers

Volunteers usually work at a level which is closest to daily life in Nepal. They work in villages or district offices in any number of mid-level positions. Villagers have a hard time understanding why anyone would want to leave the luxury of their home to come to Nepal. They have an even harder time understanding why the volunteer isn't living like a king. Since they come from overseas, they must be rich.

The volunteer, especially in the first months in the village, will be the center of a storm of observation. They will be part honored guest, part co-worker, part visiting potentate, part village buffoon. It can be a rewarding experience for everyone involved.

The volunteer's efforts to learn the Nepali language will be greatly appreciated. Nepalis see this as a true sign of interest in them and their problems, as important perhaps as the volunteer doing their job.

Some in the village may see the volunteer as a potential resource: a pipeline to a job, a contract, a position in school, a ticket to America or wherever.

*Nepal lacks almost all infrastructure and there are almost no roads or bridges.
Here people pull a friend across the Buri Gandaki River. The seat is a piece of
wood fastened to a forked branch.*

Volunteers are usually viewed as people who have come to do a
specific job: teach in schools, build water systems, plant forests.
The volunteers often view themselves as change agents, there not
only to do a job but change the way that job is done. Nepalis do not
necessarily see the need to change things, or change things in the
way the volunteer thinks they should be changed.

Volunteers, fresh from a pampered training where they are the
center of attention, are often greeted in their new office with yawn-
ing indifference. Chances are little advance notice was given or care
taken about the volunteer's arrival. Most offices feel they have
enough to do anyway. So many things 'fall through' in Nepal, often
there is no preparation until something actually happens – permanent crisis management.

Experts

Experts often work at the central level, in Kathmandu, with periodic field trips. Their contact is mainly with the mid- and upper-level Nepalis, in their office and in His Majesty's Government, that are concerned with their project.

Personal relationships are important when working in Nepal. A business meeting will start with a round of tea and what may seem like 'small talk' to the foreigner. The Nepalis consider this a part of establishing and reinforcing the rapport necessary to get things done. The expert who pulls out his list of questions right after shaking hands may be viewed as too brusque and disrespectful of the Nepali he is meeting with.

Part of the expert's credibility from the Nepali standpoint will be

A foreign expert on the left talking to a group of farmers. The average Nepali farmer is poor and very conservative. It takes a long time to build up the necessary rapport to get them to listen.

judged on his knowledge of Nepal and Nepali culture. Someone who demonstrates an interest and knowledge of Nepal and the Nepali language adds to their standing (partly because so few experts seem to do this). Language in particular will earn extra dividends, taken by Nepalis as an indication the expert is serious about helping Nepal. Even a minimal amount of Nepali can open up discussions and get a dialogue going.

Some Nepalis may feel frustrated and belittled by the fact that they hold the same degree or qualifications as the expert, but only get a fraction of the renumeration. Travel allowances are often where these differences become most evident.

The expert has to walk a fine line, content to travel at the same level as his counterparts, willing to pick up more than his fair share of the expenses (in many circumstances the amount paid is based partially on the ability to pay). Nepalis often try to earn a little extra income by saving as much as possible on travel allowances. Experts shouldn't undercut this by staying in the most expensive places.

It's only natural that Nepalis look for ways within the project to further themselves and their family through jobs, scholarships, observation trips abroad. The expert is getting good money, regular paid vacations, education assistance for their children. Nepalis know all this, and feel they should get the same.

Working with Government Counterparts

Nepal was never a colony and Nepalis are justly proud of this. They are sensitive to foreign experts coming in and giving directions rather than consulting with them to work out a consensus.

Many bureaucrats treat their job as their own private kingdom. When a person is away from their desk, their job stops. If their stamp is needed on a paper, no one else knows where the stamp is. If their approval is needed, there is no one to give it in their place.

Your government counterpart will have a different perspective on the project. It may be only part of their duties within their government job. Their priorities and concerns will be based on their total job and their position in their own office structure. This can lead to very different viewpoints, scheduling, and objectives from what you may have. Be aware of your counterpart's viewpoint, do not dismiss them out of hand as being politically motivated or unreasonable or too slow or whatever. Stop for a second and look at things from their point of view. Look for areas of compromise, be willing to accept their viewpoint sometimes.

CROSS-CULTURAL RELATIONSHIPS
The Tourist

Tourists do not have a good image with officialdom in Nepal. Tourists really started coming to Nepal, particularly Kathmandu, in the mid-1960s. Those who came at that time were by and large 'budget travelers', the original flower children and hippies. Lured by the incredibly cheap prices, easygoing atmosphere, and the legal (and cheap) marijuana and hashish, they stayed, and stayed, and stayed.

Many of them became semi-permanent residents. Barefoot, unkempt hair, tie-dye vests and baggy pants, half-saddhu, half-smuggler; these were not part of the image Nepal wanted to project as it became more and more involved in the world community.

Badgering officials and scamming to get visas, involved in any number of somewhat dubious enterprises to get money, some of the 'hippies' became a problem. With limited experience and resources for this type of thing, the government decided to get rid of all of them instead of sifting the good from the bad.

The axe fell about 1975, at the time the present King Birendra's coronation brought Nepal into the world news for the first time. Visa regulations were tightened, hash and grass became illegal. Those without money to leave were even helped out.

The hippies as a large community disappeared. The final blow, perhaps, came in the mid-1980s when new visa regulations mandated tourists show proof of exchanging US$5 per day (now US$10) for a visa extension. The budget Shangri-La was gone, although a new generation of yuppies still marvels at the bargains.

The other major changes in tourism are the growth of group tours and the extension of the tourist season. Independent tourists have been joined by more and more clumps of group tourists, whisked around in buses from sight to sight and surrounded by souvenir sellers like seagulls and a school of fish.

Tourists used to desert Nepal in the monsoon, but group tours in particular have made tourism a year-round business recently. There is even some trekking in the monsoon now.

The Trekker

Trekking got started as people ventured out to get a closer look at those beautiful mountains and valleys. Facilities were non-existent, but to some, that added to the adventure and charm. Organized trekking began when Colonel Jimmie Roberts, who broke his leg on the only (and unsuccessful) expedition to climb Machhapucchre, opened Mountain Travel in 1965.

Trekking growth has been so rapid there is now growing concern about the negative environmental and cultural impact of the trekkers. More areas are being opened to trekkers to relieve the more heavily congested areas. Most of the northern border area and the more remote sections of the country remain closed. This is partly because of the sensitivity of the Chinese about movement along the border with Tibet, but also because of the inability of the area to feed and support its own population, let alone tourists.

Power Dressing

The hippies are gone for the most part, although you still see a few wandering around. Their memory lingers on though, and tourists and trekkers should remember that when they have to visit any Nepali office.

Think of meeting with Nepali officialdom as applying for a job. Like applying for a job, you're trying to get something. Would you apply for a job in a ragged T-shirt and barefoot? Remember that it's vacation time for you, but it's office work for them.

By dressing like a fine upstanding yuppie, you also show the person you're meeting you respect them and their position. You are maintaining their ijjat and that is important, too.

Patience

For some reason many people instantly become short tempered in the presence of bureaucrats in the third world. The rigmarole of forms, standing in line, checking, questions, another line, paying a fee, another line, coming back in the afternoon; things we have all gone through placidly at home, suddenly drives us up the wall.

The clerk you are dealing with knows little English and has a terrible time understanding what you want. Keep calm and keep smiling. Remember public displays of temper are avoided by Nepalis. If you aren't satisfied, ask to see the person's supervisor. If you have a legitimate, but touchy, point, it may be simply a question of getting to a high enough level on the bureaucratic chain so someone will take responsibility for acting on your case.

On The Trail and Tour

Respecting Nepali customs and culture makes your visit a pleasure for both sides. Tourists' ignorance can be misinterpreted as arrogance (and really, it is a form of arrogance) and conceit.

Respect for Nepali culture covers everything from walking around temples clockwise to not throwing the tissue you use to blow your nose on the side of the trail.

Two of the main areas that Nepalis, both in the city and the rural areas, disapprove of are the tourists' revealing clothes (this applies to both men and women) and their lack of respect for Nepali bathing customs.

Grin and Bear It

Almost everything the tourist eats has to be carried in from a roadhead that can be days or even more than a week away. The person cooking the food never even heard of baking powder two years ago. They never saw a tourist until five years ago, and their English is what they've picked up from tourists.

Things are not easy for the average Nepali lodge owner. It's a whole new world they're trying to cater to, a whole new world they have to learn.

Don't be surprised if sometimes your pancakes are soggy, if you get tomato soup instead of potato soup in a crowded lodge.

Sometimes there is cause to get upset, but before you do, stop and think things through first. And remember that Nepalis don't solve disagreements by intense face to face confrontations.

DEVELOPMENT WORK

Until the mid-1950's Nepal was basically shut off from the outside world. Aside from the ruling clique, the only people who had any contact with the outside world and other ways of life were the Gurkhas, the famous mercenaries who served in the Indian and British armies around the world.

King Tribuvan and his government were basically starting from scratch when they overthrew the Rana autocracy in 1951. Each area had a *mukhya*, a direct appointee of the king (the Ranas) and its own bureaucracy that also depended on royal patronage.

Local authorities were given responsibility with little real power or decision-making authority. Questions went straight from the district to Kathmandu, with almost no regional integration. Keeping the country broken into small pieces made it easier to control.

Until 1953 there was not even a national budget. The national treasury was the same as the Ranas' private bank account. If it was a choice between that Italian crystal chandelier and a new school, well, there were no books for the kids to read anyway. Instead of

The town of Khandbari in the east. It is the administrative center of Sankuwasabha, one of Nepal's 75 districts. It is about two days' walk from the nearest motor road. The streets are paved with large stones.

any real planning, a notice was simply sent to each district stating how much it could spend (and how much it was to collect).

In the Terai, land was in the hands of powerful *zemindars*, absentee owners, many of whom had received the land as a grant from the king for loyal service. Until the Land Reform Act of 1955, all the land in the country was officially held by 450 families.

Land reform didn't get any 'teeth' until 1964, when ownership ceilings were established (2.67 hectares or 6.6 acres in Kathmandu, 4.11 hectares or 10.2 acres in the Middle Hills, and 17 hectares or 42 acres in the Terai). In spite of an on-going effort, land reform is not complete and there are still large numbers of landless and tenant farmers in both the Terai and Middle Hills.

In 1952 Kathmandu finally got a road connection to the outside world with the completion of the Raj Marg to India. Before that there had only been a few stretches of road in the Terai and the Kathmandu Valley. Cars for use by the Ranas had been carried over the passes into Kathmandu on great rafts of porters' backs. In 1955 there was a total of 624 kilometers (387 miles) of road (everything from paved to dirt). Road service to Pokhara was not opened until the 1970s. As late as 1974 only six trucks a day were arriving in Pokhara.

Even the East-West Highway across the relatively flat Terai will not be completed until the mid-1990s. There are now about 6,000 kilometers (3,720 miles) of road throughout the country, with less than half paved.

Regular air service didn't start until the mid-1950s using Dakota DC-3s. In 1953 the start of air service to Pokhara introduced the first wheeled bullock carts there (to load and unload the planes). Today a number of airstrips service remote areas of the country with regular flights (depending on the weather) by Twin Otters carrying 16–21 passengers.

Education was almost non-existent. A 'progressive' Rana prime minister's attempts at educational reform in the early 1900s were quickly quashed by other members of his family. At the time of the Rana overthrow, Nepal's literacy rate was about 10%, with that of women about 5%.

Health care was largely through jankris, traditional faith healers who had little or no knowledge of modern medical techniques. Pokhara, the largest and most important town in the Middle Hills after Kathmandu, didn't have a doctor until 1959.

Nepal is justly proud that it was never anybody's colony and managed to avoid being just another native principality in the British Raj. Some Nepalis will tell you privately it may have been better if they had been in the empire. At the very least, like India, there would probably be more of an infrastructure and a stronger civil service, both of which Nepal needs even today.

A LOOK AT DEVELOPMENT AID

Nepal's movement toward joining the modern world actually started before the restoration of the monarchy when the Ranas, feeling the pressure for reform, established diplomatic ties with several countries in an attempt to strengthen its claims of legitimacy.

King Tribuvan quickly expanded these ties and signed a foreign aid agreement with the USA (one of USAID's first projects was to develop a national budget process). In the early 1950s, at the height of the Cold War, the big boys jumped on the domino bandwagon and the USA, USSR, India, and China were all actively funding aid to Nepal. Each built a section of the Raj Marg from Kathmandu to India and east to Bhiratnagar.

Large socialist-style signs marking the bridges on the Soviet section of the road proclaim the friendship of the USSR and Nepal, but friendship is about all the Russians give these days. Although they maintain a very large embassy compound surrounded by high walls, their aid is almost negligible.

India, China, and the USA are still large and active donors, but the Japanese have taken over as the main bilateral donor. China is

A project agreement signing. The Nepali officials are dressed in jackets over 'dara-sarwal', the Nepali national dress for men, and 'topi', the national hat. The Westerners wear ties and sports jackets. Ties and jackets are only necessary for occasions like this one.

not only a donor: in recent years it has developed into a major supplier of contractors to build various aid projects throughout the country.

This occasionally causes friction with India, the other Asian superpower. When a Chinese contractor was on the point of being awarded the contract for a major highway bridge in far western Nepal, India objected strenuously on grounds the project was too close to the Indian border.

Almost all the developed countries of Europe as well as the European Community itself have aid programs in Nepal.

The United Nations is represented by the UNDP, UNICEF, WHO, FAO, ILO, and UNESCO. The World Bank is a major supporter of Nepal and so is the Asian Development Bank.

There are more than 30 NGOs (non-governmental aid organizations such as CARE, Save the Children, Action Aid, and World Neighbors) and the number is still growing. Most of these work under the auspices of the Social Services National Coordination Council (SSNCC).

The SSNCC, formed in 1977 under the chairmanship of the queen (she is no longer chairman), also includes over 150 national organizations. Affiliation with SSNCC means funds must be channeled through the council.

In 1976 the World Bank took the lead in forming a donor group, the Nepal Aid Group, that meets annually. In 1983, the Ministry of Finance was persuaded to form a local organization of donors to ease discussion and communication between the government and the development community.

Even with these attempts at coordination, there is still a bunch of different people saying a bunch of different things about aid in Nepal. Each agency, each government operates with its own philosophy and its own system for accomplishing it.

Project agreements are signed at the central level in Kathmandu, but implementation happens at the district and local level. It often becomes apparent that the local administration has not been consulted and has little idea what the project is expected to do, what the local administration is expected to do, and how they are expected to do or administer the project.

To the local administration the project becomes just one more on the long list of projects they're under pressure to complete, with only half the people they need to do it.

Development Budget

In the 1984/85 budget, development expenditures totaled 65% of Nepal's national budget of Rs 8,395 million. Government revenues paid 47%, 21% came from internal loans, and 32% from foreign aid grants and loans. From 1986, 40% of the budget came from foreign sources.

Whether this foreign aid has been effective or not is a question that will never be answered and will always be controversial. Nepal has had continuing problems absorbing foreign aid. Implementation of projects has often been hampered by the inability of the economy to process and spend the funding. The government has taken some steps, including structural changes, to strengthen its ability to manage and implement large amounts of development funds, and its performance is improving.

Infrastructure projects, particularly transport (roads) and power, continually get the largest shares of development aid. In the years from 1980/81 to 1984/85, 19% of development aid went to transport, 18.8% to power, and 13.8% to irrigation projects.

Although issues like high infant mortality and the need for greater education are given high visibility, Education received just 5.3%, Health 4.8%, Drinking Water 3.1%. And even though deforestation is constantly named as an enormous threat to Nepal's environment, Forestry received only 3.8% of the development budget (other agricultural projects received 13.2%, with the remaining 11.4% going to Industry and Commerce).

Major donors tend to favor large projects that can consume the large amounts of funding they have to give. Major infrastructure projects like roads and hydroelectric plants enable aid agencies to use the large blocks of funds they must expend to satisfy their overseeing bodies.

Large infrastructure projects have the added plus of having high visibility, both in the country and in the development community.

Alternate Views

Whether the economic and development benefit of these projects is equal to the large amounts of capital needed for them is increasingly being questioned. Several studies have shown that roads and electricity are not the sure path to economic and social development they were once supposed to be.

New criteria such as environmental impact and cultural consequences are being used to judge development projects. Some evaluations have been critical of large-scale projects, finding they do not have the purported results and are more detrimental than beneficial. A small but growing body of development critics, both Nepali and expatriate, are offering alternate views through various channels including journals such as *Himal* magazine.

In the 1980s, 'People's Participation' became a must in all development proposals. Just how the people should participate has not been defined and people's participation is a nebulous, but almost mandatory, part of development projects. People's participation may be given just perfunctory acknowledgment in some projects, but others are using it as a legitimate tool to strengthen their project. The 'Annapurna Conservation Area Project' is an example of a project planned and implemented with rigorous involvement of local communities.

Credibility

Development has taken some hard knocks in Nepal. It has not been able to live up to the lofty expectations set for it. These days villagers are cynical and suspicious of the next claim or promise after watching so many previous ones fail or simply fade away.

A water system is promised, a year later a survey team spends a night in the village, two years later the villagers are still waiting. A mini-hydro is built, but only large enough to supply 60 watts to each home. There's nothing left to power machinery or cook food. The drain on forest resources continues and the economy is unchanged. After a year the turbine is damaged, a year later it hasn't been repaired.

Corruption also became a problem in the 1980s. It comes in many forms. Some of it is good old-fashioned graft: bribes, kickbacks, accounting tricks. But some of the graft is harder to pin down.

A bilateral project pays a government accountant a bonus for doing its work, even though the project's funds are going through normal government channels and should be part of the accountant's normal duties.

A district assembly president is flown to the sponsoring country for an 'exchange visit'. He gets his ticket changed to go through Hong Kong and uses his travel allowance to buy a TV, a video deck, gold, and a few saris.

A high official in Kathmandu requests a just-arrived project vehicle that should go to the project site in the Terai. The vehicle never comes back and can be seen on the streets of Kathmandu ferrying children to school and waiting while someone's wife does her vegetable shopping.

These are some of the forms corruption takes.

In Your Office

Nepal is a very hierarchical society, where authority is respected and deferred to. There is not much in the average Nepali's upbringing to encourage them into taking any initiative. You're taught to know your place and stay there, deferring to those above, ordering about those below. Education is the same, stressing acquisition of raw information without putting any importance on how to apply it. Variations from the text are not encouraged and are in fact often discouraged. All this carries over into the workplace.

It is most apparent in government offices. You are told what to do or you are telling someone what to do. Your desk is your own little fief and you reject all suggestions from outsiders on how to do your work more effectively.

In Kathmandu, the pool of people who have contact with Western-style offices either through study abroad or through working experience with expatriates is expanding all the time. Still, expats in Nepal may find their position very different from that in their office back home.

People working in the head office in Kathmandu sometimes feel the fact that they work in Kathmandu gives them an additional step up the ladder over people working in the field. A job in Kathmandu is given more status than a job in the field, and the same goes for the people filling those positions.

Ideas

In a meeting with project staff, a request for ideas or new approaches to a problem is met by awkward silence. The expat starts the discussion and waits for reactions, but there are none until he starts asking directly for some. Some desultory discussion goes round and round saying something, but saying nothing. The expat, to open up discussion more would say, "Well, how about if we did...?" Expecting feedback, he gets only a few minor questions. Everyone agrees that's the way to do it.

It is not that the staff don't have ideas, you can believe they do. It is not really a matter of self-confidence, either. Staff have more than enough self-confidence. It is more a question of position. The expat may view the meeting as a group of people gathered to solve a problem, but his staff see it as a meeting of the staff organization chart, with only you at the top.

People are reluctant to make a move or statement that could be interpreted as outside their position. Doing this could get them in trouble with the staff above them for usurping their turf or for making the superior lose face by saying or doing what was the superior's to say or do. This is especially true in a public meeting where the people involved are face to face.

When the expat makes his suggestion, as the highest-ranking person, of course it should be accepted. To question or reject it would cause you to lose face. To cause you to lose face could threaten your evaluation of the worker and whether he gets that raise or not.

Drawing opinions from even upper-level staff in an open meeting can be difficult. They may simply defer to you or clam up when they hear your opinion. As time goes on, if open meetings are a regular feature, some more open discussion may occur, but in general there is a reticence to express opinions in meetings.

Staff may be much more forthcoming in one-to-one meetings where they feel confident that what they say is not openly public. In meetings though, the emphasis is on maintaining everyone's ijjat and the smooth relations (at least in public) of the staff.

Intercaste and Group Relations in The Office

Decision Making in Village Nepal by Father Casper Miller discusses an incident in which a low-caste Sarki being cheated by a Brahmin asks another Brahmin with whom he is on good terms whether he should accept what the first Brahmin says. The two Brahmins have no connection or relationship whatsoever. The Sarki and the Brahmin he asks for advice are from the same area and have a long and friendly relationship.

The second Brahmin knows the first one was lying and would cheat the Sarki badly. He stands to gain nothing from the profit of the first, too, but still the Brahmin backs up what the other Brahmin has said and the Sarki is duly cheated.

The bonds of caste win over the personal relationship one has with people of other castes.

The bonds of caste usually play a detrimental role in office relations as well. The expat may hear about a 'Newar Network' or 'Brahmin Clique' from someone who feels it is disrupting the office or feels he is being victimized by it.

Whether or not the expat sees any friction or conspiracy, whether or not he believes there is anything, his Nepali staff do. There may be nothing, or the person may have been a victim, as the Sarki was, of a casual, momentary alliance based on caste and circumstances rather than an office Putsch in the making.

These charges (and countercharges) usually involve Brahmins, Chhetris, and Newars. They are nothing new. These three groups were vying for power for centuries long before the first project

195

agreement was signed in Kathmandu. Traditionally they are the only three groups who received education and had the qualifications to hold administrative posts.

There has been an effort to make education universal and bring all Nepal's various castes and groups into administrative and high level positions, but Brahmins, Chhetris, and Newars still hold the majority of posts.

There is not much that can be done about charges like this. Certainly the more diverse the background of the office staff, the less likely charges like this are liable to be heard. The charges almost always have their roots in the actions of an individual, and any action taken should be taken on an individual basis.

The Emerald City

A job in Kathmandu seems to be like Dorothy's Emerald City in the film *The Wizard of Oz*: once you make it to Kathmandu, all your problems are solved. Field postings, even for people who only came to Kathmandu later in their life, are often viewed as an exile to Siberia.

People want to get to Kathmandu for professional and personal reasons. The only way to get ahead professionally is to be in Kathmandu. Out of sight, out of mind. The boss can't see you if you're not there, you can't develop those important personal relationships in the office, you can't hear about those new jobs and chances for overseas study trips out in the field.

On a more personal level, a posting in Kathmandu means a chance to put the children into Kathmandu schools. Most people feel the schools in Kathmandu are the best in the country, and everyone wants the best for their children. If a person is posted from a job in Kathmandu to a job outside Kathmandu, chances are they will leave their family in the capital, especially if they have school-going children.

Staff Friction

Friction often occurs between the field staff and head office staff, the result of poor communications, disparate work situations, and wide differences in living conditions.

Difficulties of communication can lead to frustration on both sides. People in the field feel the head office has forgotten them, people in the head office feel field staff are permanently on tea break.

In any project a strong communications setup is a necessity. Regular visits by head office staff to field sites are essential. There is no substitute for seeing things first-hand.

There is a good chance that upper level staff, particularly administrative staff, have spent little time in the field. It is surprising how many of the staff have never been outside the Kathmandu Valley, or only leave for a once-a-year visit at Dasain.

With little experience in the field, Kathmandu staff have a habit of showing little understanding, sympathy, or patience for problems in the field. Problems which emerge from the field are treated as non-problems or ignored, left to a puzzled field staff.

Kathmandu staff have a tendency to get enmeshed in their own rut of paperwork and meetings. The field becomes an abstract form, another report to read and secondary in importance to pushing papers and getting to that meeting.

In the Nepali government your job is your kingdom, a valuable property that gives you whatever power you have. To share your job while you're in the field is to risk losing that power.

This mentality often carries over to development office staff. My job is my turf. Sharing of knowledge and training, the idea of having a co-worker to 'cover' when someone is out, is not common. If someone else knows my job, they may try to take it or the boss may say I'm no longer needed.

A last reason why some staff may be reluctant to go to the field is the poor accommodations and food available in the field. A question of status may be involved, too. A high-ranking staff may feel it is beneath their position to make a trip to the field unless it's in a helicopter. 'Roughing it' is for junior staff.

Expatriate Field Trips

These problems are not unique to the Nepali staff. Expatriate staff may hear the same types of excuses from other expats and they will sometimes hear themselves making the same rationalizations. It's only human nature to give the problems on your desk higher priority than problems that are days away and only hazily understood. But it is important to make that effort and get out.

If your office cannot function without you there for the week or two you're in the field, then there is something wrong with your office. Don't make (or imagine) yourself so invaluable.

By taking a field trip you are building relations with your home and field staff. Your staff will be more willing to go out if they know that you've made the trip too. If you don't make regular trips to the field, you are putting up one more small barrier between yourself and your Nepali staff.

Many high-ranking Nepali staff almost have to be dragged screaming out into the field, and junior staff don't like it either. Nepalis are well aware of the double standards for pay and benefits between expats and themselves, and resent an expat who orders staff to the field while ducking out themselves.

It is important for the expatriate to make regular field trips to the site and arrange regular trips for their superior if possible. Nothing gets things moving like a visit from a high-ranking staff, particularly if you are perceived as being a direct representative of the funding agency.

Nagging questions get cut through, the field staff get a big morale boost, the whole project gains legitimacy in government district offices. The project gets a new momentum that carries on long after the expat has left.

In The Field: A Chicken Everyday

If a staff member is hired or transferred from Kathmandu to a field position, most offices have some kind of field allowance or 'up-country allowance'. Staff on field trips are eligible for daily allowances, one of the job's 'perks' and a valuable source of income for lower level staff.

Staff used to the good life in Kathmandu often complain of the privations of the field and may do their best to live at Kathmandu standards. Field staff may spend half their day worrying about arranging for the nightly chicken demanded by visiting head office staff.

The Kathmandu staff feel they are roughing it and making the best of a bad situation, but local people and local staff grumble about people who come and act like visiting royalty.

Staff on field trips should not be expected to sacrifice their health through inadequate nutrition, and if a trip to the field is pure drudgery, they will be doubly reluctant to go the next time. At the same time, staff visiting in the field should be sensitive to the living standard of the local people, the local government staff and most importantly local staff from their own office. They should act and live in a manner that is compatible with the local situation.

EXPRESSING CRITICISM

Nepalis do not like to express criticism of others in public. The emphasis on maintaining smooth public relationships seen in rural society carries over to the urban office. Open criticism of fellow workers, or another department or project, is rarely voiced.

Nepalis prefer to criticize in private. This may mean a one-to-one conversation, perhaps in the office with no one around or over a cup of tea in the local tea shop or even during an early morning call on a morning walk.

Criticism is made indirectly, told to one person with the knowledge that that person will relay the criticism to the person concerned. By expressing the criticism without face to face confrontation, embarrassment and animosity are avoided. But, without the restraining presence of the person being criticized, the criticism can sometimes grow into a general condemnation.

What started out as a complaint on the person's slowness in completing a report can build into a complaint of everything the person does right down to the maddening habit of clearing their throat every time they speak.

When hearing such complaints it's a good idea to take what's said with a grain of salt. This is as much blowing off steam as anything else. The listener must separate the real criticism and let all the steam blow away as if it was never heard.

When hearing such criticism it's also a good idea not to hold it against the person doing the criticism.

Nepalis are taught not to confront people, and to wait until the point can be made in an indirect fashion. That can take some time. Pressure builds up and when it blows, there can be a big bang. It's a good idea to plug your ears sometimes, or pretend you didn't hear anything.

DISCIPLINE

To be disciplined or scolded in public is very degrading for a Nepali, a blow against their ijjat. If a staff member is criticized at a meeting, they may deeply resent the fact that the criticism was given in public even if the criticism was fair. They may resent the public embarrassment so much they forget about the original criticism.

Nepalis are often reluctant to take direct disciplinary action. They often feel that criticism alone is punishment enough, that no punishment such as a loss of grade or pay is necessary.

Further action, including firing, is taken very reluctantly. Once a person is given a job, it is very difficult to get them removed. As long as no one is hurt directly, Nepalis seem more tolerant of poor job performance and human foibles than most Western managers.

You may hear complaints about someone, but it is very rare to hear anyone saying a person should be dismissed, and still rarer to find anyone taking that action. By complaining loud enough (indirectly), or shifting their responsibilities or posting, perhaps the troublesome employee will get the message, find another job, and simply leave. That leaves everyone's ijjat intact, the best resolution to the situation.

In cases where money has been taken or misappropriated, disciplinary action may seem very light by Western standards. In one case, an accountant caught embezzling pension funds was allowed to pay back the money and keep his job. In another office, a storekeeper/general service officer was allowed to simply resign after being caught stealing thousands of dollars from the agency.

In neither of the above cases was any civil action taken or the police even consulted. The most severe penalty for most cases is simply the loss of job. Little can be done to recover the money lost.

Again, the concern seems to be with preventing any open, public situation. If a case is made against someone, that person may make counter charges against other people in the agency in an attempt to save face and shift blame. The result could be very messy and take a long time to settle. Better to quickly and quietly resolve the problem so things can get back to normal as soon as possible.

HIRING

An advertisement for a position in the local papers, any position, may receive several hundred respondents. Chances are many of the applicants are qualified. Thanks to improved education and increasing opportunities to study, the pool of educated people is increasing. Unfortunately it is increasing at a much faster rate than the job market is able to absorb them.

Résumés or bio-datas may include a thick sheaf of photocopied documents and certificates to prove that the person really did attend the schools and obtain the degrees they say they did.

There may have been 300 applications and 50 first-round interviews, but that does not stop the unsuccessful applicants from complaining about not getting an interview and raising charges of nepotism and discrimination.

Age vs. Youth

Much of what happens in Nepal happens because of personal connections developed through family, friends, school, and work. These connections are built up through the years. A person who knows who to call and when to call them is a valuable asset to any office, even though they may sometimes forget where a car and driver are every once in a while. Thus most companies prefer to employ older people who have the necessary connections.

Staff Relations

Many Westerners keep photos of their family on their desk, but talk only of family matters with other staff in the most general terms. Nepalis, used to village and neighborhood life where almost everything is common knowledge, are much more willing to discuss their family life. Many Westerners draw a line between home and office.

Most staff will know the personal situation of the other people in the office: their spouse, kids, what school they go to, how everyone's health is, which doctors they use, how their home construction is going on, any connections they have. It's similar to life in a small village where everyone takes a very healthy interest in everyone else's business.

Your staff will feel much more comfortable working with you if they have some knowledge of you not only as an office staff, but as a person as well. It's not that you have to hand out biographies of everyone in your family, just be willing to answer questions about yourself and your family, and don't give the impression that your family is not a proper topic for discussion.

Even a small reciprocation by you of their interest will also go a long way to building strong staff relationships. Stepping into some section's office in the morning for a few minutes of small talk on the way to your own office, taking a question to them rather than calling them to your office all the time, an occasional staff party, all will go a long way to help good rapport with your staff.

That doesn't mean you have to be everybody's buddy. You should just show a willingness to listen and respond within the parameters of the office staff structure: this is all it takes. Don't disappear into the 'expatriate ghetto'.

OPEN DOOR POLICY

Be prepared for 'open door' management. Westerners like closed doors guarded by secretaries, hold the calls, and answer one question before going on to the next. Nepalis are used to offices that seem like community meeting centers. A Nepali sometimes has to leave his own office to have a private conversation. While your office is in no danger of becoming like that, you should be aware that offices in Nepal are not sacrosanct, and Nepalis are used to and expect much freer access to offices of even high-level officials than a Westerner would.

Of course high-level offices in Kathmandu function like a standard Western office, but in the districts, and at mid-level offices in Kathmandu, be prepared for a variety show happening during your visit.

Over 90% of Nepalis come from villages. It's an oral society with a very low literacy rate. When you have a problem, you talk it out, usually with every neighbor around listening in – memos and written documents simply don't work.

Also, authority in Nepal is often very centralized and even the smallest things have to be approved at a very high level.

That's what Nepalis are used to, and it's what they bring with themselves to the workplace. Your staff will appreciate knowing they can talk to you just about at will, without being told to come back later because you're in the middle of writing a report or without being yelled at for bothering you for such a small matter.

If you do keep your door shut repeatedly, tell people to come back later. Your staff will probably think you're a little strange and maybe not such a good manager, since you can only think of one thing at a time.

IN NEPALI GOVERNMENT OFFICES
Open Management

Someone walking into a Nepali office for the first time may think they have walked right into the middle of pandemonium. Especially in district offices, but even in mid-level Kathmandu offices, it may seem that 10 things are happening at the same time, none of them particularly quickly, but all of them involving lots of conversation and consultation.

In most Nepali offices, the office and the waiting room are one and the same; your business is conducted in front of any number of other people. As your problem is being discussed, someone else walks in and sits down. After a few minutes he starts to comment on your conversation. A clerk walks in with a sheaf of papers for the boss to sign. He talks to the clerk while you talk to the other man, even though you have no idea who he is.

An overseer comes in and asks the boss for a travel advance. Another man comes in the office and hunkers down in the corner watching. You talk to the boss a few more minutes until the peon comes in with a note.

Two men follow the note in and are soon in a deep whispered conversation with the boss. Two more men and a policeman come in and start another conversation. Soon everyone is around the desk talking and the boss peers around the corner of the crowd and asks you another question. The overseer comes in for another signature.

Somehow Nepalis make all this work. Remember the speaker's floor goes to the most persistent and loudest voice: offices like this

are no place to be shy. If you want your problem solved, be forceful. Every time someone brings up a different subject, work to bring it back to yours – this is no place for a polite 'after you'.

Slower Pace

The office can seem chaotic, but work actually moves ahead at a slow pace. There are no computers and electronic mail here; you're lucky if there's a typewriter, luckier if there's a typist. Everything seems to require approval by at least two unconnected (and often absent) bosses. Letters can take weeks to reach their destination and if there's the slightest error, they may not be honored.

Dispersal of funds requires approval by both the auditor general's office and the ministry receiving the money. Neither office seems to be concerned with the needs or schedule of the other. All funds are frozen a month before the end of the fiscal year and take months to unfreeze again.

OFFICE HOURS

Government offices are open six days a week, with Saturday off. On Friday, offices close at 3 p.m., but other days they close at 5 p.m. and open at 10 a.m. In winter offices close at 4 p.m.

There has been much talk of converting to a 5-day, 9 to 5 week, but so far it is only talk. People complain that it would ruin the morning meal: it would be too early to be able to prepare a meal, much less enjoy it.

As it is, most offices don't really get rolling until 10:30 or so. There is a 20-minute tea break at about 1 p.m. that gets stretched considerably, and people start disappearing well before 5 p.m.

Non-office Hours

Because of the chaos and lack of privacy in government offices, much work is done before or after normal hours by dropping in the home of the person needed in the early morning or after office hours. This is a traditional way of working throughout Nepal and no one objects to the mix of office work and private life. Some people prefer to sneak off for a cup of tea together after work to discuss that nagging problem.

Courtesy Calls

Arriving in a district center, it is courtesy to go not just to the office you're concerned with, but to step in and see all the high officials in town. This may involve several cups of tea as you make the rounds, but it's worth it. Your visit may only last a few minutes, but it's much easier than having the bosses find out who you are through the grapevine.

If it's your first time in an office, carry a proper letter of introduction from your counterpart ministry or office to help establish yourself and give you some clout in the field.

The Peon to The Rescue

One of the most valuable people in government offices is also one of the lowest paid. The peon takes the place of all the electronic gadgetry and modern labor savers of Western offices. Poised (or dozing) outside the boss's office, roused into action by the brrrrrrrrrring of the wind-up bell on the boss's desk, they do everything from fetching tea and cigarettes to delivering a letter across town to chasing down disappearing staff and bringing them to report to the boss.

The peon is much more valuable than their duties would indicate. There are few people who understand the far-from-tidy office landscape better: where a file is at any moment, where it goes next, where a particular staff goes for their tea break, alternative ways to do some bureaucratic procedure, who is easy to work with, who should be avoided, what local people to consult, where to get the best tea, food, raksi.

Having the peon on your side can cut the time it takes to move your file through an office or get your questions answered. Get on the wrong side and your file stays at the bottom of the pile, the staff you need to meet can't be found, a porter can't be found to carry your luggage.

Treat peons with the respect they deserve. If you order tea, get them one, too. An occasional cigarette, a friendly word, giving them a little recognition is all it takes to make your job move faster.

Documents

Letters and documents are treated with a mix of respect and suspicion in Nepali offices. A proper letter of introduction, a letter authorizing some action to be taken can make things go much easier on field trips. Improper documents can cause more problems than if you had nothing at all.

Make sure you have all the proper documents and that they are neat with no major mistakes or crossed-out sections. Most importantly, make sure all documents are properly stamped with the seal of the issuing office. This stamp can mean all the difference on whether the letter or document is accepted or not.

Out in the district five or six days' walk from Kathmandu is no place to find your authorization to disperse project funds isn't honored because the letter from your office lacks the office stamp and your ministry has mispelled your name on your letter of introduction.

– Chapter Eight –

CLOSE ENCOUNTERS

MORE RICE?

The Unexpected Visitor

It's 6:45 a.m. and you're lying in bed just waking up. You hear a call from outside. You throw on some clothes and get to the door. Outside is Ram Bahadur, dressed for the office.

Ram Bahadur is a young mid-level government technician for a district office that is working on one small field site of your project. He's just come in on the night bus from the field. "Good morning sir," he says brightly, and then waits to be asked in.

You remember you said he could drop by and see you next time he was in town, but...

He has just been called by his office to Kathmandu, but he would like to talk to you about that possible observation trip to the Philippines and a position he has heard will be opening in your office in Kathmandu.

After tea and toast, through long pauses that leave you uncomfortable, he remains smilingly seated. You don't want to be a bad host, but you hint that you should be getting ready for the office, ask where he's staying, hint he needs to drop his things off before he goes to the office. No, he says, he's going straight to the office.

After a long pause in the conversation, he picks up a magazine and begins thumbing through it. Finally you get up, excuse yourself, and rush to get ready for the office.

At 8:45 it's time for you to head for the office, and you offer to drop Ram somewhere. He accepts, and in the car makes one last appeal for the job in the office and the observation tour.

Nepali visits are not goal-oriented, less worried about long pauses and 'dead time'. And in a country where communicating by phone is still unavailable to most of the population, calling ahead is usually not an option and not often trusted even when available.

People just go. If the person they are visiting is out, they'll wait. If that person will be out a long time, well, Nepali people are used to waiting a long time.

Conversation is welcome, but there is not the feeling that people should be talking all the time. Long pauses are acceptable and a normal part of conversations. Moments spent staring into space or at the latest issue of *Time* magazine are not a signal that your guest is bored stiff.

Nepalis do not make a strict separation between home and business. This visit could have taken place in your office, but then the whole office would have known about it and Ram would be questioned about why he wanted to see you. Ram doesn't want word getting around he's applying for the trip or the job.

Early morning visits like this are quite a normal way for Nepalis to discuss business. It is often the only way they can get some quiet, uninterrupted time to talk. With Nepal's open office system, early morning visits or after office snacks together are about the only chance people get to talk things over privately.

ENTERTAINING

Most Nepali visits start with a round of milk tea; in hot weather a cold soft drink may be welcome. High caste Hindus may decline offers of beer or hard drinks because of their dietary restrictions, so it's a good idea to have soft drinks on hand, too. But don't be surprised if your Brahmin guest does ask for a beer or a whisky and soda. They may have developed a taste for it while studying overseas. Most women ask for tea or soft drinks.

When entertaining, remember that some of your guests may have dietary restrictions. Beef is out for everybody, some may be vegetarian, and some Brahmins may decline to eat rice in your house. You should have several varieties of food so that there will be something for everybody. Chicken is about the safest meat to serve.

Nepalis run into this all the time. There is no need to get too nervous about offending someone if you give things a little thought beforehand. There's no need to put flags on the dishes; if your guest is concerned, they'll ask. These restrictions are a part of their everyday life and, as long as you respect them, there's no need to make a big thing out of them.

After The Party

Most middle-class Nepali families do not have access to a car. Buses stop running by about 9 p.m. and taxis seem to disappear about the same time. Those that are available charge at least double the fare and are very choosy about where they will go.

If you are lucky enough to have a motorcycle or a car, part of your responsibilities as the host may be to take your guests home. Of course they will say they are OK and you don't need to do this, but if you don't take them it could mean an hour or more walking for them.

Many Nepalis, after leaving some evening function with a meal included, or after leaving (and eating some dinner at) an expatriate's home will go straight to their own home and have a meal of dal-bhaat-tarkaari. This doesn't mean they didn't like your food, it's just that they don't feel (and their wife doesn't feel) they've eaten until they've had rice cooked in their own home.

Instant Invitations

An invitation may be delivered to you as late as the very day of the function, and often invitations are delivered only the afternoon before the function. (This is also true for office functions: seminar opening and closing ceremonies, workshop graduations, etc.)

Invitations for formal functions (a rice feeding festival, a brata-bandha, a wedding) usually arrive on 5x8 inch (12x20 cm) cards. There are printing shops everywhere that do these and they can custom print just about any type of invitation needed. The invitations are usually hand delivered.

Cocktails

In district centers, the men of the office you work with may have a welcoming (or farewell) party. These will usually start in the early evening with a group of men from the district offices, possibly some local school teachers or the local headmaster.

Many of these men are probably not from the area, but have been posted there by their offices. Often wives and children are left behind in Kathmandu or in the man's real home. These civil servant cliques are a common feature of district centers. A part of the evening may be spent listening to their laments about being posted to such a remote area.

In a room, blankets or mats will be spread on the floor and everyone sits in a circle using the wall as a back rest. Beer is either not available or prohibitively expensive except in major Terai towns. Kukhuri Rum (made in Nepal) is a standard drink, sometimes vodka or gin (also made in Nepal) may be served.

Most common of all is raksi, locally made liquor usually dis-

'Raksi' is the favorite drink in Nepal. This young Gurung woman dressed in typical clothes is selling raksi from the wooden jug next to her.

tilled from kodo (millet) and liberally cut with water. It tastes best slightly warm.

Snacks may start out with *dalmut*, made from deep-fried lentils, often with peanuts and peas mixed in. They come in varying degrees of spiciness and saltiness.

After some time curried meat will probably start to arrive. Chicken or *khasi* (castrated goat) are most common. If the chicken has been killed just for this occasion, as is often the case, a plate with the insides (heart, liver, etc.) will be served first.

Remember the prohibitions on jutho when eating and try not to let your fingers touch your mouth as you eat. If there is a small spoon, even if it is given to you personally, do not put the spoon in your mouth. Use it to drop or pour the food into your mouth. If in doubt, watch your neighbors.

SORE LEGS

You may notice the office peon acting as the server. As he moves about in the circle, he walks hunched over, careful not to touch anything with his feet and never lifting his foot more than is absolutely necessary to move, lest his foot steps higher than anything or anyone.

No matter how tired your legs get, be careful not to point them at anyone as you sit. Your hosts will be very understanding of the lack of limber in foreign legs, but don't abuse this courtesy by pointing them at someone. If there is no way to avoid it, drape something over your feet to cover them.

If you need to get outside to relieve yourself, avoid passing through the circle of guests. Walk behind people's backs, being careful not to hit them with your foot or lift your foot very high. It is quite acceptable to ask someone to shift forward.

Where's The Food?

The drinks keep coming, you've eaten a ton of snacks, and still there's no sign of the food. Sit back, relax, have another glass, have some more snacks. The meal is only eaten at the very end of the party in Nepal. If people are having a good time, they won't ask for rice till 9:30 or 10. It's the kitchen's job to keep the food warm and ready until then.

When everyone has eaten, the party is over. Almost as soon as everyone has washed their hands, people head for home. The party ends with the eating of rice. There is no custom of drinking tea or coffee after the meal.

When traveling in the hills, a supply of dalmut or some other snacks and a bottle (or two) of foreign whisky come in handy and are guaranteed to make you a most welcome guest.

In A Country Home

If invited to a rural home, you will probably be invited to sit on the raised porch that serves as an outdoor room in most Nepali households and given a woven mat or a wool blanket to sit on.

Everybody in the household will find a way to catch a glimpse of you and within five minutes a small child will probably be leaning against your elbow. Expect tea or raksi to arrive. Raksi is given just about any time, tea only until early evening.

Where you are served the meal will depend on what caste of people your host is. If your host is upper caste Hindu you may be served outside on the porch. This is to prevent pollution of the kitchen. Even if you are allowed inside the house, be sure to stay out of the area where the food is actually cooked. You may eat alone too, or just with the friends who have come with you, if your Brahmin host decides to eat in his kitchen.

Hill tribes are more likely to invite you into the house. Watch what other people do with their shoes. When in doubt, take them off.

You will be served by the women of the family usually, and will probably have to ask for some of the rice to be removed from your plate. Your hosts will be happy if you ask for more later, but

A typical home in a Himalayan village: the stock of wood is for the coming winter and the fodder on top of the wood is for the livestock. The woman is spinning wool into thread from which she will make the family's clothes.

whatever is left on your plate is thrown to the animals. So don't be shy about having a small appetite.

Urban Homes

In urban homes there may be chairs to sit on. However, socializing habits are the same as in the country: drinks and snacks, rice (food) served only when the drinking is finished, everyone leaving soon after finishing the meal.

The woman of the house may not be around much, busy with managing the kitchen and the meal. She may not eat with you. Urban homes may provide you with a spoon to eat your dal-bhaat-tarkaari, but if you want to eat with your hand, that is fine, too.

Somehow it always tastes better if eaten with the fingers.

ABSORBING THE SHOCK: SETTLING IN
Visa Regulations
You can get a one-month tourist visa from Nepali embassies and consulates. On the way to Nepal this can be done in Hong Kong, Bangkok, Singapore, Delhi, Calcutta, Dhaka, or Lhasa. The fee is US$10. You will need at least two passport-size photos and it will take at least one night to process.

Alternatively, you can receive a two-week visa on arrival at the airport. Have a passport-size photo and US$10 handy. This visa can easily be extended another two weeks for no additional fee.

The immigration office for visas and trekking permits is in Thamel near the SAARC office. There is a bank right inside the office. During the tourist season (October-April), the office can be terribly crowded. It is open from 10 a.m. to 5 p.m., and it's a good idea to be there before 10. There is another office in Pokhara near Ratnapuri, but this office can only grant two-week extensions.

Your visa can be extended a second month for Rs 300 or Rs 75 per week. For a third month the fee is Rs 600 or Rs 150 per week, for a fourth month Rs 900 or Rs 225 per week.

Tourists who wish to stay longer than one month must show a receipt from an authorized moneychanger to prove they have changed US$10 for every day they intend to stay in Nepal.

At the present time it is possible to spend up to four months of any calendar year in Nepal.

Trekking Permits
For trips outside of Kathmandu, Pokhara, Chitwan or places en route, a trekking permit is required. Trekking permits cost Rs 60 per week if you've been in the country less than two months and Rs 75 beyond that. Trekking permits are issued at the immigration offices

A trail scene in eastern Nepal with a typical village behind. You will often encounter Nepalis taking a rest from a long walk. The checked blanket beside this Rai man indicates he is on a long trip.

in Kathmandu and Pokhara. The Pokhara office can only grant 15-day permits.

Applications are color coded. Make sure you have the right color and, in Kathmandu, make sure you're standing in the right line. You also need to show proof that you have changed US$10 per day.

If you have a trekking permit, you do not need to apply again for a visa for the same period.

Long Term Visas

It is very difficult to stay more than four months per year. People who are working in Nepal must have documentation supporting their application from both their own organization and their counterpart Nepali organization and/or concerned ministry.

The attitude toward long-term stays and foreigners working in Nepal in general has stiffened considerably in the last several years. Approval is no longer automatic. Most visas for projects are given for one year at a time. Extensions are also being given more reluctantly. A four-year project term no longer means a four-year visa for the expatriate expert position named in the project.

Customs for The Casual Tourist

Photographers are allowed one camera body and the usual assortment of lenses, but a second camera body is usually not a problem. Bringing in more than 20 rolls of film may be a problem.

Video cameras technically require a special permit, but tourists are usually allowed to bring them in with few problems. The customs officer may want to make a note in your passport to ensure the camera leaves the country with you. Bringing in more than a few video cassettes is difficult.

Exit Customs for The Tourist

It is illegal to take any statue or art object more than 100 years old out of the country. The export of any statue or art object that looks even a little bit old requires a certificate from the Department of Archaeology. The shop you buy the article from or your travel agent can help you with this.

Carpet regulations on Nepali wool carpets change from time to time, so ask around first. Customs officials may ask to see proof you have changed sufficient money to buy the carpet. There is no problem exporting the silk Kashmiri carpets also found in Kathmandu.

Customs for Long-Term Stays

When you pack, make a careful, detailed list of each item in each box. Carry a copy with you on the way to Nepal. It may seem like a lot of work, but it can save you time and trouble clearing customs or if anything is lost.

There should be someone from your office to help you. Sea freight is very slow and of questionable reliability. Most people send their things as unaccompanied baggage and by air freight.

Bring a knife to open any boxes the customs officer wishes to inspect and a roll of wide, heavy tape to close those boxes. Bring all your keys and a copy of the list of items in every box.

The customs warehouse at the airport can be chaotic. It may take you all day or more to complete customs procedures. Much of this time will be spent simply waiting. Take someone from your office, have the detailed list of the contents of each box, and pick up a peon to help you as soon as you arrive. He will help locate your baggage, find porters to carry them out, locate the customs officer, and generally shepherd you through the different forms and offices. There are no carts or tractors, everything moves by manpower. Be prepared to tip the peon and the porters who carry your boxes.

You are allowed to bring in just about anything you will need for your household. Clothes and small items are usually no problem. You are usually allowed one each of any major electric appliances. In my experience, the more detailed the list, the less inclined the customs officer is to try and work his way through it.

It is possible to buy appliances duty-free through several commercial agencies in Kathmandu. These usually come from Hong Kong and are compatible with Nepal's voltage. Also it is usually easier and more reliable than trying to ship your own appliances, and easier to get it serviced.

Importing A Car

Regulations on importing cars have been changing, so make sure you get the latest regulations from your office before you decide to do it. If you intend to import your car, be aware that Nepali roads (and drivers) are very rough on cars. Most people who bring a car choose to leave it in Nepal when they leave.

Nepalis drive on the left of the road. Parts for American cars and most European cars are not available. Importing parts for them can be difficult, will take a long time and is usually expensive.

It is possible to order a new car through several dealers in Nepal. Once ordered, it will take 2–3 months to arrive.

There are usually a few duty-free cars up for sale among the expatriate community in Kathmandu. When buying a used car, it is very important that all the paperwork, including the original import documents and all subsequent sales papers, be properly documented. Have the documents checked before you buy the car. Discrepancies may mean the car's duty-free status is invalidated. With duties of 100% and more, this can be a very expensive surprise.

Parts for Japanese cars, especially Toyota and Nissan, are the most readily available. For all other cars, parts are a problem.

Exit Customs After A Long Stay

The Nepali government keeps a file of all duty-free purchases. Prior to leaving the country the expatriate must be able to show whether the items are being exported or sold. The expatriate may be held responsible for any duty due. The shipment of their other belongings may be held up until these duties are cleared. In practice, however, this mainly applies to cars.

Everything will have to be cleared at the airport export warehouse prior to being sent out as unaccompanied baggage. Make a detailed list of the contents of each container. Most shipping companies have agents right at the warehouse. Do not seal your boxes before taking them to the airport. Have your lists and documents ready for customs inspections.

The export of any statue or art object over 100 years old is strictly prohibited. The same regulations as for the tourist apply here. The customs officer may also ask to open it (or other objects) as some of these have in the past been used to smuggle drugs.

Bring heavy duty tape or plastic straps to seal your containers after inspection. The shipping company's staff will help you.

Clothing

Except in the Himalayas, Nepal has a temperate climate. In Kathmandu in winter, early morning lows are about freezing, but after the morning fog burns off it gets quite warm, with outside temperatures climbing to the low 20s C (low 70s F). Inside temperatures stay cool, which is why government staff are often found sitting outside.

Keep a warm wool sweater handy. Nights can get very cold. Down vests are useful, too. Anyone who will be out above 2,000 m (6,000 ft) in the winter will probably want to have a down jacket.

Riding a bike or motorcycle feels great in a T-shirt during the day, but sweaters and down jackets are necessary after sunset.

The rest of the year you're more worried about keeping cool, and cotton clothes make the most sense. In the hot season before the monsoon (from April to June), temperatures can reach the low 30s C (high 80s F) and cool to the high teens C (low 60s F) at night.

The pre-monsoon and the monsoon are quite humid. Cotton is the most comfortable thing to wear. Umbrellas are invaluable for keeping the sun and the rain out; hats hold the sun off.

It can get quite cold in the hills and shawls are a favorite of both men and women in the cold season. This little girl is sitting over the hole of a stove, warmed by the glowing embers below.

Tourists in particular should remember that Nepali people dress conservatively. Halter tops, tank tops or short shorts on women and men are not acceptable. Most women find hiking in a knee length skirt more comfortable and practical than shorts or pants. It is definitely more culturally acceptable.

Men should not walk around bare-chested. Pants, shirt and decent footwear should be worn when meeting a government official.

Unless you work in an embassy, ties or dresses are not necessary at the office except for special ceremonies, seminar openings, and receptions. Dress is casual in offices, but conservative.

What's Available

All types of clothing are available in Kathmandu's bazaars. Stores on New Road and in the Supermarket area have all kinds of ready-made clothes. But they are expensive for the quality available. All kinds of shoes are also available, even Nike high tops, but these are expensive too, and sometimes seem to be 'seconds'. For cheap Nepali ready-made clothes, head for Thamel.

There are dozens of tailors around and dozens more shops stacked high with bolts of cloth. You can get everything from fine Hong Kong wool tweeds to cheap Indian cottons. Any tailor will happily copy your favorite shirt at a low price; but for suits and jackets, it's best to go to a tailor recommended by someone you know.

A number of women's boutiques on Kantipath and Durbar Marg cater to Western tastes. They use a wide variety of fabrics: cottons, silks, wools. They have their own designs or will work to your specifications.

A much wider variety of children's clothes has become available in the last few years, but prices are still high. Children's shoes are

A typical Middle Hills bazaar scene: a snake charmer from the Terai entertaining the crowd. With no TV or cinema, wandering shows like this are still a major source of entertainment.

hit or miss. You may find the right type of shoe, but not the right size. Move on to the next store and try there.

The Thamel area has all kinds of new and used camping and 'outdoor clothing', for which you will pay about the same as if bought new back home. Check what you buy very carefully.

If you are going on a trek, you can rent everything you need from shops in Thamel at very reasonable prices. Renting used shoes or boots is often buying someone else's blisters. It's best to bring your own.

WHAT TO BRING

If your office doesn't provide you with them, most appliances are available in Kathmandu. They will be expensive and should be checked carefully first. If you have duty-free privileges, you can order them through any number of agencies. They usually come from Hong Kong and are for Nepali voltage.

Nepal's 220 volt, 50 cycle electricity is very unreliable. Not only are there frequent power blackouts, but there are almost constant fluctuations in the voltage. At any moment you may have 200, 230, even as low as 170V. This is especially true in winter, when electric heaters and cookers are widely used.

You will need some kind of voltage stabilizer for your major electric appliances: refrigerator, TV, VCR, hi-fi systems, and any-thing else that can be affected by voltage fluctuation. You don't need one for every appliance. Stabilizers come with several wattage capacities: 500, 1,000, 1,500, and more. Several appliances can be run off one stabilizer. Bring a handful of plugs, both male and female, to help with any wiring adjustments you want to make. Extension cords are handy too.

Stoves and Ovens

Many expat homes cook on gas stoves. The irregular supply makes kerosene back-up stoves a necessity. Two types are available: an

VACUUM CLEANER. MULTI-SYSTEM TV AND VIDEO. DOWN
JACKETS. SWEATERS. PLUGS. EXTENSION LEAD. BOOSTER.
SHORT WAVE RADIO. SOLAR BATTERY CHARGER. LOTS OF
FILM. POTS AND PANS. VOLTAGE STABILISER. VIDEO HEAD
COTTON CLOTHES. KNIVES...

Indian stove you pump to maintain pressure on a jet of burning
kerosene, or a second type that uses a ring of wicks and air convec-
tion to maintain a good flame. The pressure stove is much noisier
and, because it requires preheating, is not as clean.

In the major towns in the Terai you may be able to get natural
gas, but everywhere else only kerosene or firewood is available.

Some Nepalis use an electric coil mounted in a ceramic base to
cook, but these are unadjustable, inefficient, often don't work because of the 'brownouts', and frequently blow fuses or melt wires.

In the bazaar in Kathmandu, it is sometimes possible to find a
simple oven to place on top of your kerosene stove. Small electric
ovens and oven toasters are available in the bazaar or may be
ordered through duty-free agents.

Television and Radio

Nepal's television is on the PAL system. Almost all the rental videos available are on the same system. If your home country's system is not PAL, consider buying a multi-system television and video deck. These are available in the bazaar, but are expensive. It is a good idea to bring a spare head for your video deck. The rental video tapes are very tough on your VCR and spare parts are hard to come by.

Antenna boosters are necessary to get a good picture and to have any hope of receiving Indian television. These are best bought outside Nepal. Bring a supply of antenna cable too.

Everything from walkmans to boomboxes to 1,000 watt monsters are available in the bazaar, but they are expensive. It's best to bring what you need with you. There is one AM station, Radio Nepal, and no FM. The shortwave airwaves are always full and it is a good idea to have a shortwave radio.

If you live where there is no electricity, consider investing in a solar battery charger, and bring spare chargeable batteries. A walkman uses up the cheap AA batteries available in the hills almost as fast as you can put them in. A 'battery box' is a simple device for running a walkman off a group of D-batteries. These are available in New Road audio stores.

Other Appliances

Vacuum cleaners are not available in the bazaar, and washing machines are a relatively new idea. The average upper middle-class Nepali family has someone who washes the family's clothes by hand. Many expatriates do this as well. It's a good source of employment and a way to put some money into the economy. However, washing machines are becoming more common in Kathmandu expat houses, and can even be bought in some New Road shops now, as well as through an agent.

In The Kitchen

Pots and pans are available, but are mostly made of thin aluminium. Consider bringing some of your own with you. Good kitchen knives are also hard to find. All types of crockery and silverware, mostly of Indian manufacture, are easily bought in the bazaars of Kathmandu. Bring a good quality can opener.

Photography

Nepal is a photographer's paradise. Be sure you bring a lot of film. Black and white processing and printing is available and very cheap, but quality is spotty. Find a shop you like and strike up a relationship with the people. Ganesh Photo is a long-time favorite.

Many major studios now do E-6 slide processing, but this is expensive and quality control has never been a strong point in Nepal. One hour print processing is available on New Road.

The keys for buying any photographic equipment in Kathmandu are know your prices and check your dates. Prices can vary greatly and no equipment will be cheap. Check around before you buy and know the price back home. Before you buy anything like film or batteries, check the date. Things past the expiration date have a way of turning up in Kathmandu photo shops displayed as if they were still valid. Even Kathmandu's biggest photo stores do this. Be careful.

FINDING A HOME

Your office may have a home or apartment or a selection of homes and apartments for you to choose from. There are a number of real estate brokers floating around, too. Their commission is one month's rent. Some brokers have offices, others just show up at your office.

In the past years, there has been a building boom of massive mansions specifically aimed at the expatriate market. House rents have risen dramatically, in part driven up by development agencies willing to pay based not on the going rate, but some agency formula.

There is a dual price system on apartments, one for Nepalis, another higher one for foreigners.

Your monthly rent may be equal to six months of your cook's salary, a whole year of your night watchman's. In such a poor country, who else but foreigners could afford these monstrous rents?

What's Available

Homes in Kathmandu are mostly concrete, sometimes made of brick covered in plaster. If you rent a house, expect a compound surrounded by a brick wall, a big, boxy design, walls painted sometimes in strange colors, terrazzo floors, big windows covered with security grills, and bedrooms without built-in closets.

Hot water is provided by 'gizers', electric water heaters with a capacity of 30–60 liters (7.8–15.6 gallons), at each hot water tap. Solar heating often supplements these in Kathmandu now.

Bathrooms also have terrazzo floors – nice in summer and cold in winter. Bathtubs are usually not very inviting. Most have a shower over the tub. In some houses and apartments, the bathroom is the shower stall: there is a drain in the floor, and toilet seats get wet when you shower. A toilet may have a water tap next to the seat for those who wish to clean themselves Nepali-style.

There are neighborhoods with large concentrations of foreigners, but there are no real foreign 'ghettos'. There may be a crumbling brick house with a tea shop on the ground floor and a radio blaring right next to a palatial home.

Things to Ask and Look for

Water is a problem in some parts of Kathmandu. There may be lots of water in the winter, but only a trickle for a few hours during the dry season. Check in the neighborhood to see how the water supply is. Most homes have a ground storage tank and a smaller tank on the roof to maintain pressure in the house. The water must be pumped up to the tank once or twice a day.

Ask about the electricity supply, too. Electrical wiring is a concern. Check the capacity of the wiring. Are there enough outlets (there never are)? Do the outlets work? Do they pull out of the wall when you unplug something? How are the gizers? If the gizer and an iron are on at the same time, do you blow a fuse?

Check for water spots, especially on the top floor. Roof slabs are often of questionable quality and leaks can be a problem.

Check to make sure the windows open and close and can be locked easily. Green wood used in window frames often warps after it's put in. Check that the screens are in good condition and there are enough of them.

Check whether your landlord is willing to pay for repairs and painting. Find out if transportation is available for you and your staff.

Telephones

If your potential landlord says he hasn't got a telephone, but it's coming any day, be aware that you are taking a chance. People wait years for telephones in Kathmandu that are coming any day.

Furnishing Your Home

You can get just about everything you need to furnish your home right in Kathmandu, but have to go to a different store for each type of furnishing. Heavy hardwood furniture, steel desks and cabinets, and rattan furniture are all available, but it is expensive. It is easy to have furniture custom made, too, at no extra cost.

The closest thing to a department store with everything is the Bluebird at the Hotel Bluestar. It's also worth checking some of the older stores that stock Indian goods on and around New Road.

For mattresses there are a variety of plastic foams ('dunlops') available. You can also have a cotton or kapok mattress custom-made by Indians who wander around plucking what looks like a one-string harp. Bargain hard with them. You have to buy the kapok and the cover material separately. These must be dried and re-'fluffed' occasionally. Quilts made from kapok are also common. Good quality blankets are hard to find, as are sheets.

DUTY-FREE

There is a duty-free bonded warehouse across from Singha Durbar, and a variety of wine, liquors, cigarettes, and even some perfumes, are available. If you have duty-free status, you can buy here. There is a limit to how much you can buy, and agreements are different for different countries. Payment must be in dollars, and checks are OK.

STAFFING A HOUSE

It is common for expatriates working in Nepal to have some household staff. Many middle-class Nepali families have a servant, too, usually a young boy or girl from the village to wash dishes and clothes, and help with the shopping. The servant receives food, clothes, medical care, a place to stay, and occasionally some money from the family.

If you are working fulltime, and taking care of kids is a fulltime job too, then you will probably need to have some help around the house. Life in Nepal is very labor-intensive. It can take half a day just to pay the electricity bill, days to get the telephone fixed, hours in the bazaar to finish the shopping. No frozen foods here; if you want to eat something, you make it.

Most families find that some household staff can be a big help. Having staff does not mean the *saaheb* (master, pronounced 'saab') and *memsaaheb* (madam, 'memsaab') relax and lead lives of idle luxury. Servants can help you through the rough bumps and bruises of life in the fifth world, but you still have to lead the way.

With a little work it is possible to find great people to help you. Language may be a problem, but there should be efforts from both sides. Learning Nepali is a good way to strengthen your personal relationship.

Responsibilities of The Saaheb and Memsaaheb

The relationship between you and your household staff is more complex than a straight employer to employee one.

Staff normally work a 6-day week, with Sunday off. It is up to you to negotiate exactly what hours and responsibilities are. Time off should be given at Dasain. Another few days should be given at Tihar, and all major holidays or a day in lieu of the holiday.

There are usually unexpected things that come up – a special puja, or a special guthi meeting – that will require time off and a few days per year should be allowed for this type of leave. This is standard practice in Nepali offices as well.

Salary

You will be responsible for paying the staff a monthly salary. At Dasain it is normal to give a one-month bonus and a new set of good clothes. Inflation is a problem in Nepal, and if your staff is doing a good job, their salary should be raised on a regular basis.

Other Benefits

It is customary to provide fulltime staff with one meal, morning and afternoon tea, and a light afternoon snack as well. The staff can cook their own meals (dal-bhaat-tarkaari) with the food you provide them.

Besides the one set of clothes given at Dasain, it is a good idea to give some clothes to wear while working, for establishing a good relationship, if nothing else.

You should be responsible for each employee's health. This can mean bills for doctors, tests, X-rays, and any medicines. You may want to extend this to the servant's family as well. For your own health as well as theirs, give each servant a regular health check, particularly a stool test. If you believe in GG shots, get these for your staff, too.

Some people give an education allowance (as most offices do) to help pay school fees for children. If your servant is the sole support of their family, you may want to consider this.

Work

It will take some time for you to get used to each other. As well as teaching job duties, you may find yourself teaching a language, nutrition, and personal hygiene, as well. It is very important to train everyone to wash their hands with soap before they handle food.

Remember that many Nepalis have no concept of what modern appliances are, how they work, how foreigners live, and what duties they have as a member of the household staff. Have patience and a good sense of humor, don't expect everything to come easily, and expect the occasional gum-up.

Another important point is care about water, both handling it and drinking it. While they are working, it's a good idea to make servants drink boiled and filtered water, even if they drink tap water outside.

Discipline

If you are forced to discipline any staff, remember that straight, direct criticism can lead to hard feelings and more trouble later on. Don't make the person lose face in front of others. Nepalis are usually diplomatic about their criticism and accept criticism better when it is done diplomatically.

As jobs in Nepal go, working in a foreigner's house is pretty good. Still some staff try to take advantage of their situation. If you have staff, you have to supervise them: check their work, check the sums on purchases they make. Most Nepalis welcome this as insurance against any future problems.

In Nepal, the police are usually not involved unless absolutely necessary. People try to work things out themselves and only go to the police as a last resort. If you do have problems, try and work them out without appealing to the police.

MAIL

The General Post Office is at Sundara, near Bhimsen's Tower. It's open from 10 a.m. to 5 p.m. (4 p.m. in winter), but don't expect much to happen before 10:20. Stand in one line to get the letter weighed and find out how much it costs, another line to buy stamps, another to get the letter canceled. Be sure you see each item you mail canceled, or your letter may be 'lost'. Don't use the mailboxes around town. If you are staying in a hotel, your hotel may mail your letter for you.

Behind the GPO is the Foreign Post Office for sending parcels. Registered sea mail is cheap and reliable, but slow (3–4 months). Make sure your package is carefully wrapped.

Receiving Mail

Tourists can receive mail at the Poste Restante. It's in the GPO and opens at about 11 a.m. All the mail is there out in the open for anyone to go through. Never have anything of value sent through the mail.

People working in Nepal receive mail through their office. Magazines arrive, but irregularly and very late. It is best not to send packages through the mail.

Express Mail and Courier Service

DHL and UPS both have services to and from Nepal. As of going to print, Federal Express does not. Receiving anything other than letters through these services may necessitate applying for an import license, which can take a few days. It may mean paying customs, too.

Telephone

Domestic and international calls can be made from the Central Telegraph Office across from the stadium. You can also send telegraphs and telegrams from there. Making a call entails a long wait.

Most major hotels have telex and many hotels, even medium-sized ones, have fax machines.

If you have a telephone, your landlord must pay a deposit before international calls can be made on it. Nepal has IDD (International Direct Dial Service) and connections are usually very good. The country code for direct dialing to Nepal is 977.

Nepal has extra charges on any line there is known to be a fax machine on.

BAZAAR SHOPPING

In Nepal, you go to one shop for stationery, another for canned goods, still another for spices, buy your vegetables on the street, pick up fruit farther down, and pick up a magazine from a last store before heading home. It's a good idea to bring your own bags and always have your *jola* (shoulder bag) handy.

There are some stores, like the Bluebird at Thapatalli and Lazimpat and the Nanglo at Dilli Bazaar, that are as close as you come to a department store or supermarket, but you often pay a little extra for this convenience. Almost anything available in Kathmandu is found in the New Road, Asan Tole area. The Supermarket is Kathmandu's version of a mall and has Nepal's first (and still only) escalator.

Bargaining

You can bargain for just about anything except some staples. Don't start bargaining unless you are fairly serious about buying. Remember, if your offer is accepted, don't try to undercut it further. If you back out of buying something after a round of bargaining with your offer accepted, don't ever expect to be welcome at that shop again. A price named is considered an agreement to buy at that price.

Dual Pricing

Remember that prices in Nepal are often based on what it is felt the buyer can afford to pay. Prices for rich people, whether Nepali or foreign, are higher than for a poor Nepali. In Nepal, foreigners are assumed to be rich. Even if the foreigner is on an extra-tight budget, they are still richer than the average Nepali.

Don't be surprised or upset if you pay a little extra, just bargain harder and find out from friends what they're paying. If you willingly and knowingly pay too much, then prices will go up for everyone. You'll be adding to inflation, something Nepal needs no help increasing.

– Chapter Nine –

GETTING AROUND

Most people arrive in Kathmandu via Delhi, Bangkok, Singapore, or Hong Kong. Most flights come from these cities. There are a few flights each week from London and Frankfurt as well. It is also possible to reach Kathmandu from Karachi, Varanasi, Dhaka, and Lhasa. During the tourist season (October–April) reservations should be made well in advance as flights will be packed.

Getting from The Airport into Town

Taxis are available for about US$3 for the five-minute ride from the airport to town. There is also a shuttle bus for about US$0.50 to the major hotels and downtown Kathmandu.

All real taxis have meters, but they may be 'broken' on the trip from the airport. Make sure you settle on a price before getting in.

Domestic Flights

Tickets for Pokhara, Lukla, and the Mountain Flight are purchased from the RNAC building on New Road. All other domestic flight tickets are sold at the RNAC office in Thapathalli. Both offices can be chaotic. Service is hard to get, and so are tickets.

A much easier way of getting tickets is to go to a reputable travel agent. The flights most frequently used by tourists have a special (much higher) tourist price. You pay in foreign currency, but any refunds will be in Nepali rupees.

You can only make a reservation from the point of origin of the flight: you cannot make a reservation to fly back from Jomsom until you arrive in Jomsom. Flights are often booked far ahead. A travel agency may be able to help you around this.

Be aware that flights in Nepal are frequently delayed or canceled. Do not depend on flying back from trekking one day and flying out of the country the next. Allow yourself at least a one-day leeway.

Buses

Buses are a bargain, but often uncomfortable and slow. Local buses will get you anywhere in and around the valley for less than Rs 10. The main stations are Ratna Park and Baagh Bazaar.

Long distance buses can be tiring. The blue *Saajaa* (co-operative) buses are the best. Tickets are available at Bhimsen's Tower near the General Post Office. This is where the buses leave from, too. Bhimsen's Tower is also where several 'tourist' buses to Pokhara depart from. These are more expensive, but more comfortable and faster than regular buses.

There are night buses to and from most major centers. Sit toward the front; rear seats feel like being in a catapult sometimes.

Regular buses for Pokhara and other long-distance buses leave from the central bus station on the east side of Ratna Park. Always buy long-distance bus tickets at least one day in advance.

Taxis

Taxis have black license plates. All taxis are metered. If the driver says the meter is broken, don't take it. During daytime, just pay the fare on the meter. At night, a 50% surcharge over the meter must be given and even more will be requested. Tips are not necessary, but are often expected. It's the rare driver who has any small change. Taxis can be rented by the day, but it is usually as cheap and more comfortable to rent a car.

Cars

Cars can be rented, on a daily, weekly or monthly basis, from travel agencies. The cost of the car includes a driver. Prices are cheap when compared to those in more developed countries, but still expensive by Nepali standards.

Motorcycles

Motorcycles are available for rental at several places in Thamel and the New Road area. They're not as popular as they were a few years ago: more people are now opting for mountain bikes. The motorcycles are old, smoky, noisy, and riding them is not particularly safe in Nepal. Remember to always wear a helmet.

Bicycles

In the mid-80s, mountain bikes started showing up on the streets of Kathmandu. They can now be rented for US$2–3 a day from a number of places in Thamel. One-speed bicycles can be rented in

Thamel and Rani Pokhari. These may not have the same visual impact as a mountain bike, but for just getting around Kathmandu, they're all you need and they are much cheaper. Make sure your brakes and your light work.

Rani Pokhari is the bicycle center of Kathmandu. You can buy a Thai- or Taiwan-made mountain bike or a one-speed Indian or Chinese bike for a fraction of the mountain bike's price. There are sometimes used European and American mountain bikes on sale too. However, these tend to be quite expensive.

Outside Kathmandu one-gear bikes are about all that's available, and for parts and maintenance these are still the best ones to get.

Rickshaws

Rickshaws are tricycles that hold a pedaler and seat two passengers. In Kathmandu, rickshaws are no bargain. They are fun, but will cost you about as much and sometimes even more than a taxi. In most Terai towns there are no taxis. Rickshaws are the main mode of transportation. In any case, make sure the price is negotiated and agreed on before you get on the rickshaw.

Tongas

Tongas are horse-carts that hold about six passengers and are pulled by a single horse. They are common in some western Terai towns. They usually go on a set route, but they can also be chartered.

TREKKING AND TOURING

Independent trekkers arrange and manage their own trek. They carry their own packs, or hire a porter themselves. They determine their own route and find their own hotels, food, trails, and decide where and when to stop and when to start.

When trekking through an agency, all this is done for you. You only have to put one foot in front of the other. Porters carry your gear, your meals are all planned, you sleep in tents pitched by the staff, your guide tells you where to look, and when to start and stop.

Independent trekking is, of course, much cheaper, but agency trekking is much easier and worry-free. Independent trekkers have to worry about losing the trail, finding a hotel or place to stay (this can be a real problem in trekking season), and the knowledge that if anything happens, they're on their own.

If you are on a tight schedule and have the money, or if you just want a nice, relaxing time without fuss or bother, then organized trekking is fine for you. If you have the time and the energy, don't mind some minor hassles, don't mind being exhausted at the end of at least the first couple of days, and want to get a little closer to life in Nepal, try doing it yourself.

What to Expect

Trekking is not the same throughout Nepal. The Annapurna circuit offers the widest range of experience, both culturally and visually. The walk to Jomsom doesn't have the same great views as the Manang side, but is culturally interesting and offers the best accommodations and food you'll find on the trekking trail. The trip to the Annapurna Sanctuary has stupendous scenery at its end, and is fairly short. The Everest area offers the thrill of being near Everest, good scenery, and an interesting culture, the Sherpas. Time often determines what trek is taken, and if there is time, it'd be hard to find a better combination of mountain views, interesting cultures, and comfortable accommodations than the Annapurna circuit.

Accommodations

Most trekking hotels have foam rubber mattresses, either in simple rooms or dormitories. Walls may be just a woven mat. Electricity is almost non-existent, and hot water is usually available only after you ask for it to be heated up. Forget daily showers, hair dryers, and sit down toilets. Toilets are latrines with squat plates, if there is anything. At night the hotel may give you a simple lamp or candle.

Vegetables are still a rare thing in the hills. Here, this young man carries a pumpkin down from its rooftop storage to become part of that night's meal.

Food

On main trails carbohydrate loading is no problem. On the Annapurna trek there are places you can get everything from lasagna to apple pie to burritos to chocolate cake. Fried rice, pancakes, oatmeal porridge, and fried noodles are other trekking trail staples. Potatoes are another big item in the upper areas. Meat and eggs are available sometimes.

If you hike off the main trekking trails you learn to like dal-bhaat-tarkaari or starve. Don't worry about dieting: it would be difficult not to lose weight on a trek. You should be more concerned with keeping up your energy, so heap on that rice and dal.

Snack foods like muesli, granola, peanut butter, and the occasional chocolate bar taste great on the trail and are easily available in Kathmandu. Mints, gum and bite-size candies are welcome breaks from the sometimes bland, sometimes spicy trail diet. They may be available, but it's better to just expect to find biscuits in trail stores. Don't expect much fresh fruit.

Classes and Tours

There are dozens of Nepali Language Schools in Kathmandu catering to the expatriate and tourist populations.

Travel agencies offer dozens of tours from half day to treks lasting over three weeks. The tour guides of the larger agencies are usually very knowledgeable and full of little known tidbits about the place being visited.

The Community Service Center operating from the American Compound at Phora Durbar sponsors tours and talks on all sorts of topics conducted by long-time residents and academics studying different aspects of Nepali culture. These are open to members of the expatriate community.

SOME BASICS ON THE LANGUAGE

With over a dozen major languages in the country and dozens more dialects, about 50% of the population speaks Nepali as a second language. What this means for the foreigner is that Nepalis are used to hearing their language mangled and are quite comfortable with new speakers. If you stay in Nepal a few years and work at it, you will be able to speak the national language better than a considerable number of Nepalis.

Nepali is an Indo-European language, which has many similarities with Hindi. They share the same script and have many similarities in grammar and vocabulary.

Nepali sentence structure is very different from English. The usual word order is subject-object-verb. There are suffix 'markers' to identify the subject, object, or indirect object. The marker for the subject is *le*; for indirect object, the marker is *laai*. For example: *Chandrale Sitalaai chiya diyo*. Chandra to Sita tea gave. (Chandra gave Sita tea.)

Two different verbs share the function of the English verb 'to be'. Roughly, one form is used when describing something at that moment while the other is used for permanent states of being.

Nepali has several sounds which most new speakers stumble on. There are two 'T' sounds and two 'D' sounds that are further varied by being sometimes aspirated, sometimes not. The difference between *ka* and *kha*, for example, is difficult for us to hear or say.

Sports

The major hotels have sports facilities, usually a swimming pool and tennis courts. Some have saunas and exercise rooms, too. There are squash courts at the Oasis Hotel. The Annapurna and the Everest have billiard tables. Some of these hotels require you to become a member and pay an annual fee if you are not a guest.

There are tennis courts, billiard tables, a swimming pool, and an exercise room at the national sports center behind the stadium, that are open to everyone for a small fee.

The American Diplomatic Compound at Phora Durbar has a softball field, a swimming pool, tennis courts, squash courts, and an outdoor basketball court. The compound is for members and guests only. Membership is open to members of the American diplomatic and development community and some members of the duty-free international community. There is a membership and monthly fee.

The International Club near the Soaltee Oberoi Hotel is open to all expatriates with duty-free status. It has a swimming pool and tennis courts.

The Nepal Bridge Association holds a yearly tournament. The Nepal Kennel Association is also active.

There are two golf courses of sorts in Nepal. One is beside Pashupathinath next to the airport, the other is at Gorkarna Forest

Reserve beyond Boudhanath. Grazing cattle, horse riders, the occasional elephant, and sand for greens help to make golfing in Nepal very challenging.

There is also an active chapter of Hash Harriers in Kathmandu.

Schools

There is a wide range of preschools in Kathmandu, some of which are quite good. There is even a Montesorri School. The medium of instruction is usually English in these schools. There is often an interesting, international mix of students. Ask around and visit several before deciding.

Lincoln School is an American private school offering grades K–12. It also has an international mix of students. It is small, but has a very good, solid reputation. The alternative would be a school in some place like Bangkok or India, or in your home country.

For adult education, the American Community Service through Phora Durbar offers a wide variety of classes and lectures.

Library and Books

The AWON (A-one, American Women Of Nepal) Library across from the Himalaya Hotel is very good. It can also do with more volunteers to help in the work, too.

The British Council has a library on Kantipath open to all, with books and British newspapers and magazines. The American Library is on New Road. It has mostly non-fiction and a good selection of American magazines. The French Cultural Center in Baagh Bazaar has a small library.

Kathmandu's large tourist population ensures a wide variety of second-hand books are available in the second-hand bookstores centered in the Thamel area. Buy the book and get 50% back when you return it. Bestsellers are available in the numerous bookstores scattered around town. Prices will be the same as they are in the country of origin.

A wide variety of international news magazines are available in Kathmandu and less regularly in Pokhara. *The Herald Tribune* and *USA Today* are available and a wide variety of Indian English newspapers as well. *The Rising Nepal* is the main Nepali English daily.

Movies and Videos

Video libraries abound in Kathmandu. They mainly stock Hindi movie videos, but a few of them have a large selection of English movies and even some television shows. There is everything from children's cartoons to the latest releases to the occasional 'classic' to semi-blue movies. The videos are very cheap to rent, but that's because of the mediocre tape and copy quality.

Remember you will need a VCR and TV that accept PAL system videos to watch videos from these shops.

Pokhara and the major Terai towns have video libraries, too. The movies are predominantly in Hindi, but they may be able to get a film from Kathmandu for you.

The French Cultural Center shows a French film with English subtitles almost everyday. The German and the British Cultural Centers show films on an occasional basis.

Clubs and Organizations

American Women Of Nepal has several activities. There is another service club through the International Club.

There are many informal organizations, too. People with similar interests just get together. With as widely varied a community as you have in Kathmandu, there are people with just about every interest. It's simply a matter of asking around. Most people welcome a new enthusiast.

Rock climbing, mountain biking, bird watching, bee keeping: whatever your interests are at home, chances are you can continue to pursue them in Nepal.

The Casino

There is a casino at the Hotel Soaltee Oberoi, open all night. The majority of customers are Indian tourists. It is possible to play and win in dollars if you register.

FOOD SHOPPING

In Kathmandu, the Asan Tole Bazaar and the large vegetable bazaar in Kichapokhri are the main centers for fruits and vegetables. In the last decade the quantities and quality of vegetables have really jumped. Everything is seasonal, with prices rising and falling according to availability. You'll see lots of strange vegetables and greens; ask around to find how to cook them.

The Asan Bazaar is also a good place to find spices, flours, lentils, dried beans, raisins, walnuts, almonds, dates. You can also find *tofu* (bean curd), duck eggs, and eggs from hens not fed chemical feeds.

The Kichapokhri area has lots of dry goods and canned goods stores. In these stores it is also possible to buy frozen and fresh meat and frozen fish (from India, shrimp, pompry and some larger fish, too). Fresh fish are available here on the street, but be careful. One of the oldest and best stores in the area is the Fresh House. At Christmas they even sell candied fruit to make fruitcake.

For dairy products, there may be a dairyman in your neighborhood who will deliver. Water is always mixed in the milk. Boil it before you use it. In Kathmandu, in an alley behind Bir Hospital, is the New Nepal Dairy selling plain and sweetened yogurt, milk, and a variety of cheeses: cheddar, camembert, mozzarella, and a spice cheese. Supplies are low in the dry season. The fresh butter from here is much better than the frozen, often slightly rancid tasting butter imported from India.

In the Thamel area are a few bakeries selling different breads and delicatessen-type sausages and meats. Yak cheese is available at many of the dry goods stores. The Nanglo is well known for its bread and baked goods, and the five-star hotels all have bakeries. In the Patan area the German Bakery down the street running east across from the Narayani Hotel is excellent.

Each neighborhood has its own dry goods store and vegetable vendor, but for the greatest variety, head for the main bazaars.

The Bluebird in Thapathalli and Lazimpat and the Nanglo in Dilli Bazaar are supermarkets without the produce section. They offer the convenience of one-stop shopping, but at higher prices.

Banking

The Standard Chartered Bank, Indo-Suez Bank, and Nepal Arab Bank all have offices on Durbar Road. Gridley's Bank has an office in Baneswar near the Everest Hotel. These banks are the most convenient for banking or just changing money. People with duty-free privileges can open a convertible account. You can put in hard currency and write checks in either Nepali rupees or US dollars. But you can't put in rupees and write dollar checks.

These banks only operate in Kathmandu. The two national banks, Nepal Bank Limited and Rastriya Banija Bank, have offices throughout the country, but in the hills the nearest bank may be a few days' walk away.

Credit Cards

American Express has an office just off Durbar Marg. It is possible to make up to a US$1,000 traveler's check with a personal check and your card. They also hold mail for cardholders. Just around the corner is Annapurna Travels, the representative for VISA and Mastercard. Major hotels and the stores in them accept major cards, but most other places don't.

The Black Market

There is an active black market in hard currencies in Nepal. Changing money on the black market usually gets a much higher exchange rate than the banks. The black market was one reason the government imposed the US$10 per day regulation for tourists. If you want to use the black market, be aware that most of that money ultimately goes to fund smuggling, largely by non-Nepalis, and does little to help Nepal or the economy. You don't have to look for black market changers, they'll find you.

PETS

Many Nepali homes keep a dog as a pet or watchdog. There is no problem bringing a dog into the country and no quarantine period. There is a government veterinary clinic in Tripeshwar. There are a few private clinics, too. In the late 70s a disease almost wiped out the cat population, but cats are making a comeback now. Generally Nepalis don't like cats much, associating them with witches and black magic.

You will have no trouble bringing your pet into Nepal, but you may have trouble getting it back into your home country when you return. Most countries require certified proof that a dog has received vaccines not less than 30 days and not more than one year before returning. There will probably be a quarantine period.

There are several shops in Kathmandu selling aquariums and supplies, and tropical fish from India and Thailand.

Chapter Ten

ADJUSTING TO NEPAL

AN A-Z OF CULTURAL ADJUSTMENTS

- Affection between men and women, even married, is seldom expressed. Public kissing, hugging, and hand-holding are offensive to most Nepalis and a sign of low morals. But it is acceptable for two men to walk hand in hand.
- Anger is best not expressed openly. It causes you and the person you're mad at loss of face.
- *Bakshish* is an extra payment for a service performed and is usually given to porters or laborers at the end of the job. It can be money or clothes or anything else, and there is no set rate.
- Bargaining is to be expected. Don't bargain if you're not really interested. If your price is accepted, don't try to back out, and don't try to get an even lower price.
- Bathing in the hills is very conservative. Men should wear shorts, women should wear a lungi pulled up under the arms.
- Children are spoiled crazy. Don't be surprised if yours are the center of attraction everywhere.

- Clothing is conservative. Men should not go bare-chested and shorts should be conservative. Women should avoid bare shoulders, halter tops, and shorts. Ties and suits are not necessary except for special occasions.
- Conversations may have 'dead' patches. Nepalis are not uncomfortable with silence.
- Cows are sacred. They go and sleep where they want. Watch out for them while driving.
- Criticism should be given privately.
- Eating is done with the right hand. Only accept as much as you can eat. It is good manners to ask for 'seconds'.
- Feet should never be pointed at anyone; drape something over them if you must stretch them out while sitting on the floor. Never step over anyone, and always move your feet to let people avoid stepping over you.
- Gifts are rarely given and seldom opened in front of the person who has given it.
- Heads are sacred and should be treated with respect. Never take a topi off a man's head, even in fun.
- Invitations often arrive at the last moment. Don't be surprised or offended, it happens to everyone. If you're busy, even a short appearance is enough.
- Jutho refers to food that is ritually polluted and therefore inedible. Any food which has come into contact, either directly or indirectly, with the mouth becomes jutho.
- Left hands are used for cleaning oneself after going to the toilet. It is never used to pass or accept things, whether food at the table or money with a shopkeeper.
- Maalaas (necklaces) of shoes draped around someone's neck are the ultimate insult.
- Namaste is both greeting and farewell, combined with a prayer-like gesture.
- Offices outside Kathmandu often seem to be like a bus station

with all kinds of people coming, sitting, and going at will. Expect cups of tea and polite conversation before any business. The right to speak is often based on status and persistence.

- Payment after a social occasion is done by the person issuing the invitation. Nepalis don't divide the bill or go 'Dutch'. It is expected that the other people will reciprocate at some later date.
- Rice is a religious object as well as a food of status. Brahmins will probably not eat the rice you serve them. Do not be offended and don't try to force it on them.
- *Saalo* means brother-in-law. Calling someone a saalo is very insulting because it implies the speaker is sleeping with the person's sister.
- Servants are almost a necessity for working people.
- Shoes are considered filthy. Don't ask others to handle your shoes. Most Nepalis take their shoes off at the door.
- Status is a part of life. Don't expect your junior driver to mix easily with your senior administrative officer at the office party.
- Temples should always be walked around clockwise; the same is true of Buddhist monuments and gompas. Remove your shoes before going inside. Dress conservatively.
- Time is very flexible. A person may show up at 4 for a 3 o'clock appointment. In the hills, an appointment may be a day or more late. As a foreigner, though, you will be expected to be punctual.

TAKING CARE OF YOUR HEALTH
Before You Come

Talk to your doctor before you come. You should consider getting these immunizations: polio, typhoid, tetanus-diphtheria. There is rabies in Nepal, and you may want to consider the new vaccine against it. Remember that this is not absolute protection and, if you are bitten, you must still get further treatment as soon as possible.

Consider getting a BCG for tuberculosis, which is still a problem in Nepal. If you will be living in the Terai, be aware that occasional cases of malaria still occur. There is also encephalitis (Japanese B) in the Terai during the monsoon, and meningitis is a problem in the Kathmandu Valley during the dry season. Gamma Globulin gives partial protection from infectious hepatitis.

You can get protection from all these before you come, or in Nepal at the CIWEC clinic.

You may wish to carry a syringe and needle with you for emergencies. Be sure you see any syringe and needle taken out of a sterilized pack before the doctor or nurse uses it on you.

You must be careful with your water. Only drink water you treat with iodine or see boiling yourself, or bottled water opened in front of you. Even on an agency trek, only drink water you see boiling. Use 2–3 drops of Lugol's iodine, available in Kathmandu, to purify one liter, waiting 20 minutes before drinking.

If you are going to use toilet paper, bring your own and bring matches to burn it after use.

If you have diarrhea, drink plenty of liquids. Don't start taking medicine to plug yourself up right away. Consult your doctor about medicines to take with you before you go.

Health Insurance

It's a good idea to have some kind of traveler's health insurance if you will be in Nepal for any length of time. If you are going trekking, be sure your health insurance covers medical evacuations by helicopter. Many policies don't include this unless you specifically ask for it. It's also a good idea to see if it covers medical evacuations out of Nepal. Medical facilities are getting better in Nepal, but for many conditions the patient must still be evacuated to Bangkok for treatment.

While trekking, make sure you know your policy number and have a contact number for the insurance company. It will usually be necessary to check with the insurance company before the evacuation can take place.

Altitude Sickness

All trekkers to high altitudes (above 2,430 m or 8,000 ft) may suffer altitude sickness, no matter how many times they've done it before. Even Sir Edmund Hillary experienced altitude sickness on a trip to the Everest area in spring 1991.

There are any number of symptoms: lack of appetite, headaches, sleeplessness, weakness, dizziness. Minor symptoms are to be expected. If you start to experience them, stop climbing. If they continue or get worse, descend. You cannot 'work them out' by going farther up. Give yourself regular rest days, about one for every 1,000 m (3,000 ft) up. Don't take altitude sickness lightly, it can kill you.

HYGIENE IN YOUR HOME
Food Preparation

Most diseases come from the water, so you must be careful how you use it in cooking. Don't wash the knife and then use it to cut the tomato for salad two seconds later. Food that is fried or boiled or baked and served hot is fine.

Any vegetables you use for salad and any fruit should be thoroughly washed and then soaked in iodine water (about 2 drops per liter) for about 20 minutes before cutting.

Make sure plates, bowls, glasses, and any utensils used to eat or serve food in are dry before using them.

Make sure any servants entering the kitchen wash their hands immediately (this isn't a bad habit for the family, too).

Boil any milk you buy before drinking. Scrape the film off the top of the yogurt before eating.

Water

The bottled mineral water sold in the bazaar is fine to drink. In the home most people drink tap water that they boil and filter. Boiled then filtered or filtered then boiled: it's a great topic of discussion.

Try two filters so you can filter, boil, then filter again (but make sure everyone understands which filter is which). An alternative is about 2 drops of iodine in a liter of water and waiting 20 minutes. Lugol's iodine is the only treatment for everything in the water.

Use only treated water to even brush your teeth. In the shower, that mouthful of hot water you swallow might be clean, but it might not be, too.

Most water filters, like the Puro brand, are imported from India. Inside they have one or more 'candles' that filter the water. For best efficiency these should be replaced about once a year. Clean them thoroughly by boiling them and scrubbing lightly with an old toothbrush. Do not rely on the water filter for total protection from waterborne diseases.

255

At A Restaurant, on The Road

Only drink water you have treated or seen treated with your own eyes. Some people drink the water in five-star hotels, but you would be taking a chance. Don't believe the signs posted that say it's OK to drink the water at the restaurant.

The same goes for salads in restaurants. Don't eat them.

Only eat hot food (hot, not spicy). In open tea stalls, eat only the food which is covered.

See *Food Preparation* about milk and yogurt.

Food in Nepal is often served on wet plates, water being considered a purifying as well as a cleansing agent. You may want to rinse your plate with some of your own treated water or ask to wipe your plate clean with a cloth before any food is placed in it. It is difficult to get across the idea that you want a dry plate, but it's worth the effort.

TREKKING MEDICAL KIT

On a trekking trip there are few places where it is possible to find medical care. Carry some band aids, moleskin, a disinfectant, an elastic (Ace) bandage. Some extra innersoles for your shoes are also handy.

Lomotil is commonly used to 'plug up' people with diarrhea, but remember that your body may be trying to expel something. Don't start taking something to stop diarrhea as soon as you get it. Remember the most important thing to do if you have diarrhea is to keep yourself hydrated by drinking plenty of liquids. 'Jeevan jal' is a commonly available powder to add to drinking water to replenish your electrolytes.

It's also common to come down with a cough and a cold on a trek. Nose spray, antihistamine, cough syrup, codeine (also good for diarrhea) are all a good idea to have.

Aspirin can help sore joints and help prevent and treat inflammation.

Sunscreen should be brought. The sun can be bright in the hills and extreme on snow slopes and at higher altitudes.

Lip balm and cold cream will help keep your face and hands from chafing in windy dry high altitudes.

IF SOMETHING HAPPENS
In Kathmandu

CIWEC Clinic near the Russian Embassy is staffed by Western doctors and has a good reputation. Fees are comparable to those in the United States and payment must be made in dollars. The International Clinic near the Jai Nepal Cinema is close to Durbar Marg. This is operated by a Nepali doctor with an American license. Payment can be in rupees.

The Teaching Hospital in Maharajgunj was built with Japanese aid. The Patan Hospital in Lagankhel is also a fairly new hospital. Bir Hospital is the national hospital, but it is often crowded and does not have the best conditions. Next to Bir Hospital many doctors have private clinics in the Saajaa (cooperative) building, but seeing a doctor here can mean a long wait.

To get to a hospital quick, jump in a taxi. If you call for an ambulance, you may have to wait a long time.

Outside Kathmandu

There are hospitals in most major Terai towns, of varying degrees of competence, but don't expect much.

On most trekking routes there is little medical care available and it is best not to expect any help from them. The Himalayan Rescue Association has posts staffed with a doctor in the Everest and Manang areas during trekking season.

Helicopter Evacuations

You will have to get to the nearest radio with the following information: name, nationality, passport number and method of payment of the person to be evacuated. This means insurance policy number or name of the person guaranteeing payment. Also give a description of the injuries and say whether a doctor should come with the helicopter. Give precise directions about where the person is, including altitude.

Pickup can take several days. Pickups are usually in the morning. Keep a watch, light a smoky fire and somehow mark your location.

Be aware that no helicopter evacuation can take place until payment is guaranteed. Your embassy will generally not do this for you. If you don't have insurance, they will attempt to get a guarantee from someone at your home. Helicopter evacuations are not cheap. An evacuation costs more than US$600 per hour of flight time. A whole evacuation operation can cost up to US$2,000 or more. People cannot leave the country until their helicopter bill is cleared. If you have to be evacuated to Bangkok, your departure could be delayed by this too.

In the event of death, RNAC will not fly the body out. Helicopter charter is also difficult. The body is usually cremated and this should be done in the presence of proper witnesses: police or other local authority.

DENTAL CARE

A good tooth brush is hard to come by in Nepal. Bring enough to last until the next trip out of Nepal. Floss is sometimes available in the Bluebird.

American dentists operate a clinic inside the gates of the American Club at Phora Durbar. They are excellent, charge American fees (about), and are usually jammed. You may have better luck with Dr. K.K. Pradhan, who's also good. He has an afternoon clinic at the Saajaa building next to Bir Hospital and a well-equipped private clinic at his home.

MENTAL ADJUSTING

People coming to Nepal go through four stages in their adjustment. These stages can last different lengths of time, but the cycle of adjustment is usually over by the end of the first year in the country. People working outside Kathmandu have the most adjusting to do and (usually) the least support to help them do it.

People new to the country first experience a period of euphoria. Everything is new, exciting, exotic. During this period most people are getting special treatment and support from their office and organization. You tend to overlook the negative, the troublesome, the unpleasant. You often feel extra good about yourself, too, and can't wait to get started to bring prosperity and development to this lovely, enchanting country.

During the next period those rose-colored glasses you've been wearing slip off and shatter. From the highs of living in Shangri-La, you suddenly find yourself in purgatory. The country is the pits, your stomach hasn't felt right for a week, you can't get a pizza, a newspaper, a letter. You can't bear to look at another plate of rice. There's dirt everywhere, no one understands a word you say, and the people can't do anything anyway.

You also feel bad about yourself. You feel you've made a big mistake with your life, which just shows how incompetent you are. Your office/organization seems to have forgotten all about you, too. You may be listless and feel like you aren't healthy.

In the third stage you start to regain an even keel. You see the good and bad in Nepal, in your job, in yourself. Things about Nepal and its culture interest you again, but you look at them with clearer eyes, taking in both the beauty and the ugliness. You even start to think you understand a little about what's going on around you. You start to be able to make judgments, not just react to things as terrific or terrible.

As your perceptions become more flexible, so do you. You start to sift out what is really important to you, and what you can do without. At work you begin to understand why people act the way they do. You can see what it's possible for you to do in your job, what you can give your best shot at trying to do, and what's impossible. You can look at that plate of dal-bhaat-tarkaari again.

In the final stage, you're no longer in paradise or purgatory, you're simply where you live and work. You feel comfortable. You've settled into routines in your office and personal life. Pizza would be great, but you're quite satisfied with Nepali food and are even starting to recognize different types of rice.

Just when you thought you knew about Nepal, you realize how much more there is to learn, but it doesn't bother you. Another week without mail doesn't depress you.

People living and working in village Nepal have the biggest adjustments to make and the least support while making them. But, because of this, they often make the best adjustments and have the most satisfying experiences.

CULTURE SHOCK

We are used to patterns, routines; we do things in a certain way. When we find things are completely different, we feel stress, culture shock. That's natural, at least partly instinctive. There aren't many animals that seek out a new environment. Parrots don't naturally move to the city, polar bears don't decide to give the tropics a try. It's also partly social conditioning. We are taught to do things a certain way, that things should be a certain way. When suddenly we're put in a situation where things aren't as they should be, it's natural we feel tension and stress.

It's also natural that we look for a way to do things in our old, familiar way, to get back in our own familiar patterns or try and shut out the new, strange world we find ourselves in.

We live in our compound, have servants as a barrier between us and 'out there', insist on using our language at the office, socialize only with other expatriates.

People don't make a conscious effort to exclude Nepal, but they take for granted that one of the perks of their job is to have a life as close to life at home as possible.

It's harder to shut out Nepal if we live in a village, but some of us do our best. We retreat to our room all the time, kick everybody out and lock the door, read every book we can get our hands on, pray our mail comes on time, and think of nothing but that next trip to Kathmandu.

In the short term a retreat into our own culture cushions us from some of our culture shock, but in the long term, acting like this does nothing to help us eliminate culture shock. We never lose that feeling of unease, even in the expat scene we've retreated to because we see no alternative.

Retreating into ourselves is a little like treating the symptoms without treating the problem. The only way we can really get comfortable in our new culture is to accept it, work in it, live in it, and try to understand it.

Stepping Outside
We lose culture shock by confronting it, identifying just what is so different and strange to us, examining and understanding it, and

either changing ourselves or accepting the way things are done in this new culture. We adjust to the new culture and our new situation, learn new ways of doing things. This is initially the most difficult, but ultimately it is the least stressful, because we're eliminating the cause of the stress, not simply hiding from it.

We should become aware of ourselves. Not just that I feel uneasy or tense, but why I feel uneasy. And not just to become aware of the action or incident that made us tense, but reaching further back to the roots in us that tugged and yanked to give us that uneasy feeling: what in our culture and our individual self that makes us feel that way.

That requires objectivity, the ability to stand beside ourselves and look at our actions and our character as an unbiased observer. To really adjust we have to try and see not only what makes Nepalis the way they are, but what makes us the way we are, too. That's not so easy, but it's worth it.

Next we have to start making some decisions on starting to understand, think, react, and maybe eventually feel, in ways different from before we came to Nepal.

The Middle Way

Nepalis appreciate us when we accept (and respect) Nepali culture while remaining ourselves. To feel comfortable in both cultures at the same time.

We can't love everything about Nepal, it's impossible, just like there are things about our own culture we can't agree with, either. As individuals there will always be instances when we don't agree with the way a society and culture say something should be done.

The same is true of this Nepali culture we find ourselves confronted to. There will be things we never understand fully, things we don't like or can't agree with. But that does not mean we reject the entire culture, any more than we reject our own culture.

We have to look for a middle way, between total rejection and total infatuation, that allows us to understand and appreciate our new culture (and better understand and appreciate our own).

Take The Plunge

The only way we can really overcome culture shock is to jump into the new culture and experience it. We can read and study about the new culture all we want, but the only way to really understand human relations is to take part in them, to become active members of our new community and culture. We can only truly learn and understand a new culture by experiencing it.

Work in it, speak in it, relax in it, have some good times in it, and experience some tough moments, too. While we're doing all this, we're not just doing and feeling things, we have to observe them and ourselves from a neutral corner. From our observations we make adjustments and changes to our own way of doing things.

STRESS AND COPING

While you're doing this, be prepared for some stress, especially in the village. If there is someone you can talk to, then talk about everything you can think of. But chances are there will be no one to whom you can really tell what you're going through. Keep a diary, write lots of letters. Putting things down on paper gives you some 'distance', a chance to reconsider and analyze; plus the chance to let off steam.

If you feel yourself getting 'cabin fever' – a little claustrophobic – and your usual 'escapes' don't work, take a trip to visit somebody in another village. Remember that adjusting and overcoming culture shock does not mean turning yourself into a miserable martyr. Everyone needs a break once in a while, but it's important to see the difference between taking a break and running away. If you leave for a while, even before you leave, set a schedule for coming back.

You have to sacrifice a lot of your privacy as part of village life, but every so often just go ahead and kick everybody out of your room for an hour or so and do what you want in private. You don't have to be immersed in Nepali culture 24 hours a day. There's nothing wrong with spending time in your own culture.

If your job isn't quite what you expected, remember most development jobs aren't and then make the most of the opportunity. This is probably the only time in your life you'll be able to do your own thing. If you can't find job satisfaction in your assigned job, then develop another job or hobby that does give you satisfaction.

If you're working in Kathmandu, you may be experiencing more job frustration than anything else. Talk things over with people both inside and outside the office. Find a way to forget the office, enjoy old hobbies, find new ones – like learning the language, studying old accounts of Nepal.

It's especially easy in Kathmandu to live in a 'culture capsule', but again, this is hiding, not adjusting. The only way to really lose those job frustrations is to understand what's happening and why it's happening. From that you can move on to what you can and can't expect in your job.

The same is true if you're running the family household. Find ways to get yourself involved in the culture, don't stay in the expatriate circle. There are all kinds of opportunities in Kathmandu, take advantage of them.

SOME IMPORTANT TELEPHONE NUMBERS
RNAC 220757

Banks

Nepal Bank Limited	224337
Nepal-Arab Bank	227181
Nepal Indo-Suez Bank	411231
Gridley's Bank	212683
Standard Chartered	220129

Courier Service
UPS Courier Service   225854
(c/o Nepal Courier Service)

Car Hire
Nepal Tourist Service   225508
Yeti Travels (Avis)   221234
Gorkha Travels (Hertz)   214895

Foreign Missions

Australia	Bhat Bhateni	411578/417566
Bangladesh	Naxal	414943/414265
China	Baluwatar	411740
Denmark	Kantipath	227044
Eygpt	Pulchowk, Patan	524812/524844
France	Lazimpat	412332
Germany	Kantipath	221763/222902
India	Lainchaur	410900/414913
Israel	Lazimpat	411811/413419
Italy	Baluwatar	412280/412743
Japan	Pani Pokhari	414083/410397
Korea (North)	Jhamsikhel	521855/521084
Korea (South)	Tahachal	270172/270584
Myanmar (Burma)	Patan Dokha	524788
Netherlands	Kumarpati	522915/524597
Pakistan	Pani Pokhari	410565/411421
Sri Lanka	Kamalpokhari	414192/416432
Thailand	Thapathali	213910/213912
United Kingdom	Lainchaur	411590/414588

Government Ministries
Foreign Affairs   Singha Durbar   215905-9

265

Finance	Hari Bhawan	214311
General Administration	Harihar Bhawan	521083
Forest & Soil Conservation	Babar Mahal	220067
Agriculture	Singha Durbar	215382
Home Affairs	Singha Durbar	215024
Panchayat & Local Development	Shree Mahal	521873
Health	Tekhu	215097
Communications	Panchayat Plaza	214134
Industry	Tripureshwar	215027
Commerce	Babar Mahal	223489
Labor	Singha Durbar	215609
Tourism	Tripureshwar	212776
Law and Justice	Babar Mahal	215387
Works and Transport	Babar Mahal	215347
Housing and Physical Planning	Babar Mahal	213212
Water Resources	Babar Mahal	215046
Education and Culture	Kaiser Mahal	411599
Defense	Singha Durbar	215955
Prime Minister's Office	Singha Durbar	215955

Other Organizations

UNDP	Pulchowk	523220
FAO	Pulchowk	521139
UNICEF	Pulchowk	522857
WHO	Pulchowk	521988
ICIMOD	Jawalakhel	522839
CARE Nepal	Pulchowk	521139
Save the Children Fund	Maharajgunj	412120
United Missions of Nepal	Thapatali	212179
USAID	Rabi Bhawan	211144

Hospitals

Bir Hospital	Kantipath	221988
Emergency		221119
Red Cross Ambulance		215094
Kanti Children's Hospital	Maharajgunj	411440
Maternity Hospital	Thapatali	211243
Nepal Eye Hospital	Tripeshwar	215466
Patan Hospital	Lagankhel	522266
Emergency		522286
Teaching Hospital	Maharajgunj	412505

Private Clinics

CIWEC (near Russian Embassy)	410983
Nepal International Clinic	412842

Dental Clinics

Phora Durbar (Dr Brian Hollander)	221517
Dr. K.K. Pradhan	221142

Police Stations

Police Emergency	216999
Police Headquarters (Hanuman Dokha)	211162
in Patan	521005
in Bhaktapur	610284

CULTURAL QUIZ

Situation 1

You are walking down a street or trail in Nepal. A group of the cutest kids you have ever seen, all of them barefoot and thin, half of them naked, run up to you. They surround you, some of them dancing as they smile and beg, "Hello, one rupee, *mithaai* (candy), chocolate." You:

A. Reach into your bag of penny candy, give some to each in the rapidly growing crowd of kids, and walk (then run) off.

B. Chase them away wagging your walking stick. You stop and deliver a stern lecture on the evils of begging to the first adult in the village you see.

C. Walk on, maybe repeating their begging phrase back to them. Grin and bear it as they follow you down the trail.

Comment

People who have trekked a long time in Nepal tell you that there is only begging in an area after large groups of Westerners start to visit. Nepalis who live in the area will tell you they dislike this new habit: what will happen when these children grow up?

They also dislike the foreigners who give to beggars. If you want to really help these kids, there are plenty of worthy organizations working in Nepal that depend on donations from people like you.

Lecturing the nearest adult is being patronizing and he probably agrees with you anyway.

If you don't speak any Nepali, C is your best option.

Situation 2

You take your kids shopping with you in the bazaar. They're soon surrounded by a thick crowd of smiling faces who think your kids are the prettiest things they ever saw. A vegetable seller, with a huge smile, gently reaches up and pats one of them. Your kids look a little

uncomfortable. You:
A. Hold your kids to you and lead them out of the bazaar immediately. You never take them with you again.
B. Give your kids a smile and hug around the shoulders, tell them not to worry and, as you finish your purchase, watch how the kids are. If they're still uneasy, you calmly leave without finishing your purchases. Later you remind them how much Nepalis love kids and how curious they are about them.

Comment

Nepalis love kids, their own kids or any other kids that are handy. They'll pick up and hug any baby in sight quicker than a campaigning politician. Foreign children are especially appealing to them, because they are so different.

Before you go out, you should explain to your children how much Nepalis will be curious and friendly.

If you leave immediately, you're acting like there's something to worry about, and there isn't. By not taking them again, you take away valuable experiences from both your kids and the Nepali people. Don't put your kids in a foreign community capsule, their life will be in a capsule enough anyway.

It's best just to reassure your kids. At the same time, nobody likes to be a star all the time, and there will be times when anybody will feel claustrophobic from all that attention. Encourage your kids to get out into the community, but try and be sensitive to when they have had enough.

Situation 3

In a tea shop on a popular tourist trek, you notice the Nepali sitting next to you paying a rupee for his cup of tea as he leaves. When you get up to leave, though, the shopkeeper says tea is Rs 2. You:
A. Angrily say you saw the other guy pay only a rupee, and that's all you'll pay, too.

B. Ask how much tea is, and attempt to bargain the price down to at least Rs 1.50.

C. Ask again how much for tea, and if the shopkeeper says Rs 2, you pay it and leave.

Comment

Many services and goods in Nepal are calculated based on how much the person who is receiving them can afford to pay. That's why you bargain for many things. Foreigners are richer than Nepalis.

That extra rupee is a principle to you, but it can make or break the shopkeeper's profit for that day. He has to import everything but

the water: the tea leaves, the sugar, the milk powder. The shop-keeper probably has other high costs (like firewood). The discount to local people is economics and community relations. 'Tourist prices' are hardly a phenomenon limited to Nepal.

It is best to pay the shopkeeper and leave without making a fuss.

Situation 4

You enter the kitchen and find the cook and the maid talking. Walking around the house you see the maid has finished her normal daily cleaning, but it's obvious it's time to clean the windows. Ten minutes later you go back to the kitchen. The cook is cutting vegetables, the maid is at the door talking to the gardener. You:

A. Sharply tell the gardener and the maid to get busy.

B. Call the maid over and scold her for her laziness. Then you tell

her to get busy.

C. You call her into the living room. You explain how you want the windows washed and tell her in the future, when she runs out of things to do, to come and see you.

Comment

The maid has finished her assigned work. It isn't her job to make work for herself. Her home is nothing like yours (there was not even any glass in her rural home) and she has little idea about how to manage it. On the farm, when you finish the job, you take a break.

By scolding the maid in front of others you embarrass her; by scolding her in front of the gardener, you double the embarrassment, and by scolding them together you double the embarrassment again. By scolding her in front of the cook and together with the gardener you lower her status.

Scolding her privately is not the solution either. To her point of view, she wasn't being lazy, she'd finished her work. In Nepal, initiative is not always rewarded. She is unfamiliar with foreign households, and does not know if she won't mess something up by washing the windows and get scolded again.

The best solution is C. She knows she made a mistake, but doesn't lose face in front of anybody. She's learned a little bit more about a foreign household, too. She also knows it's OK to ask you questions. It might be a good idea to review her workload, too.

Situation 5

The office storekeeper on your construction project is discovered stealing from the project – about 100 bags of cement and some tools are missing and have been traced back to him. You call in your excellent Nepali project manager and ask him to start placing police charges against the storekeeper. A week later, when you ask what's happened, you are amazed to hear your manager hem and haw before he admits nothing has happened. Maybe, he says, it's just

better to let the storekeeper go and forget about things.

You ask your Nepali program officer. He doesn't give a direct answer, but just says what a difficult process arresting and prosecuting someone is. The storekeeper has a wife and three small children, he adds, and the cement is long since gone, too. You:

A. Call the police yourself and ask them to arrest the storekeeper and you start to investigate the program officer and project manager yourself.

B. Have the storekeeper arrested and bring in a new expat as boss above the Nepali project manager.

C. Call in your Nepali project and program officers and ask for their recommendations. They recommend giving the storekeeper a chance to replace the missing stock and dismissing him if he can't. They say give him a month to do it, you say a week. Everybody agrees on two weeks.

Comment

The large amounts of aid coming into Nepal are a temptation some people succumb to. Corruption can be a problem. With the large amounts of materials used in aid projects, it isn't uncommon for some of them to disappear into other people's homes. A tight inventory control system will help to remove some of the temptation.

Nepalis are very reluctant to press charges for several reasons. You can never tell where the case will lead to. The trail could lead to government staff or politicians who could make it very difficult to finish the project.

Jails in Nepal are not pleasant and neither is being in police custody. Locking the storekeeper in jail puts extreme hardship on his whole family. In cases where their own money or safety is not involved, Nepalis are very reluctant to inflict that on somebody else.

You hurt yourself and your office if you call the police without exhausting all other possibilities first. No one will trust that they can speak in confidence to you anymore.

Option B doesn't get the cement back and everyone in the office will resent the lack of faith you show in your Nepali staff.

With C, at least everyone will see you are giving the storekeeper a fair chance, even if you don't get the cement back. The storekeeper, with no job, no chance of a recommendation, and three kids and a wife to support, is being punished fairly severely, anyway.

Situation 6

A phone call comes through from a high official of the ministry you're working with. "About that peon's position in your office, I have a nephew who is well-qualified for the job. He said he's applied. I hope you'll consider him. I'm sure he's the man for the job." Of course he means 'give my man the job'. This is the official overseeing your project. He could easily delay your work indefinitely. You:

A. Call your administrative officer and tell him to give the job to the nephew.

B. Tell the official you're sorry, but it's up to the concerned project officer and you wouldn't think of interfering.

C. Tell the official you're sure the nephew will get all the consideration he's due. Then you call your administrative officer and tell him to schedule an extra interview for the nephew if he didn't make it to the interviews, but that he doesn't have to give any other special consideration.

Comment

This is an example of 'source'. The nephew knew there was a relationship between his uncle and your office. The high official may be under a lot of pressure from his own family to get the nephew that job. This is how things work in a country with far too many people for far too few positions. You use your power to help your own, and later the favor is returned.

If you just go ahead and hire the nephew, you may be putting an incompetent dud in the job, and showing that you are susceptible to that type of pressure, just giving yourself more problems.

If you give a flat no, you may uphold your principles, but you're also not giving the official the respect he probably feels his position is due. He could make things tough for you later.

If you remain non-commital to the official, and go through the motions of an interview, chances are everybody will be happy. You've shown respect for the official and given him room to defend himself about fulfilling his familial obligations. That will help you maintain friendly relations with him. The nephew can't really complain too much, at least he's getting an interview.

Even though you don't have to compromise your principles, remember that interpersonal relationships are very important. Try not to step on people's toes. Even if it means a little more work for you now, it could help you save time in the long run.

BIBLIOGRAPHY

Tourist and Trekking

A Guide to Trekking in Nepal. Dr. Stephen Bezruchka. The best trekking guide and much more, full of all kinds of good information.
Insight Guides: Nepal. APA Publications. Full of good information and good pictures.
Nepal. Toni Hagen. Huge coffee table book with lots of serious information.
Kathmandu Valley. Robert and Linda Fleming.
Times Travel Library: Kathmandu. Jim Goodman, Times Editions.
Exploring Mysterious Kathmandu. Katherine Hoag. Step-by-step walking tours of Kathmandu.
Treks on the Kathmandu Valley Rim. Alton C. Byers.

History

The Rise of the House of Gorkha, The Silent Cry, and *The Kot Massacre.* Father Ludwig F. Stiller. Scholarly explorations of incidents and periods of Nepal's history that help put present-day Nepal in perspective.
Sketches from Nepal. Henry Ambrose Oldfield.
Nepal. Perceval Landon.
An Account of the Kingdom of Nepaul. Col. F. Kirkpatrick.
Essays on the Languages, Literature, and Religion of Nepal and Tibet. Brian H. Hodgson. The greatest Nepali scholar of his day.

Travel Accounts

The Wildest Dreams of Kew: A Profile of Kathmandu. Jeremy Bernstein.
The Snow Leopard. Peter Matthiesen. Journey to Dolpo, much more

BIBLIOGRAPHY

than a travel book.
The Waiting Land: A Spell in Nepal. Dervla Murphy.
Travels in Nepal: The Sequestered Kingdom. Charlie Pye-Smith.
Raises issues of the environment, development programs, and social
inequalities.
Annapurna. Maurice Herzog. Both the hard drudgery and high
adventure of the first climbing of an 8,000 meter peak, a great book.
Many People Come, Looking, Looking. Galen Rowell. With excellent pictures.

Cultural, Development, Others
People of Nepal. Dor Bahadur Bista.
Festivals of Nepal. Mary M. Anderson.
Bikas-Binas/Development-Destruction. A collection of columns and
articles that give another viewpoint on many development and
tourism issues.
Decision Making in Village Nepal. Father Casper J. Miller. Good
introduction to the workings of village Nepal.
*Dangerous Wives and Sacred Sisters: the Social and Symbolic
Roles of Women among Brahmans and Chhetris of Nepal.* Dr. Lynn
Bennett.
Bhaktapur: A Town Changing. Ane Haaland.
Birds of Nepal. Robert Fleming Sr., Robert Fleming Jr., Lain Singh
Bangdel.

Cross-Cultural Adjustment
The Art of Crossing Cultures. Craig Storti. A good book on culture
shock/cultural adjustments in general by someone who spent several years in Nepal.

Language
Nepali for Trekkers: Language Tape and Phrase Book. Stephen
Bezruchka.

THE AUTHOR

Jon Burbank spent about 10 years living and working in Nepal starting in 1980. He originally went there as a Peace Corps volunteer, building small cable bridges under the Ministry of Panchayat and Local Development. He then worked for CARE as manager of a project training government overseers as they built bridges in remote areas of Nepal. After that, he worked as a freelance photographer and writer before moving to Japan. He continues to make regular visits to Nepal. Jon Burbank is the author of two other books and several magazine articles on Nepal.

INDEX

Forms of address 140

G
Gifts 148, 157, 161, 251
Greetings 123
Gurkhas 24, 40, 50–1, 54, 185
Gurungs 49, 54–6, 58, 61, 109, 115, 144

H
Health 104, 188, 191, 232, 252
    insurance 253
Hill tribes 42–3, 45–6, 48–9, 54–6, 103, 109–10, 115, 120, 122, 125, 174–5
Hinduism 31–3, 38–9, 43, 45, 50, 54, 57, 77, 79, 83, 98–9, 101, 125, 130, 144–5, 168
Hindus 19–20, 30, 33, 36, 39, 42, 46, 49, 51, 56, 58, 63–4, 68, 70–3, 78, 83–5, 107, 109–110, 115, 120, 137, 139, 154, 174, 211
Homes 215–6
Hospitals 257
Housing 228–9

I
Ijjat 119–20, 122, 184, 195, 200–1
Indra 87–8, 159–60
Invitations 212, 251

J
Janai 38–40, 107, 109, 175
Jankris 51, 53–4, 188
Jutho 43, 74, 170, 172–5, 214, 251, 259

K
Kathmandu Valley 18, 20–1, 23, 51, 70, 77–8, 83, 87, 91, 154, 158, 160, 187, 197

Khas 20, 33, 39
Khukuri 46, 51
Kiratis 18–9, 51, 115
Kitchen 74, 175–6, 228
Kumari 19, 65, 160

L
Licchavis 19, 39
Limbus 19, 51–3, 111
Loans 44, 164

M
Magars 51, 55–6, 115
Mahabharata 18, 20, 79, 83–4, 144
Mail 234, 260–1
Mallas 20, 72, 78
Manangis 60–1
Marriage 34–5, 38, 40, 48, 55, 78, 108–10, 112–3, 116, 121–2, 124–6
    arranged 113, 115
    child 36, 108, 114
    intercaste 73–4
    negotiations 113, 115
Meals 170
Meetings 194–5
Mela 110–1, 115, 154–5
Middle Hills 12–4, 17, 20, 34, 46, 50, 57–8, 67–73, 78, 166, 168, 187–8
Milk 44, 86, 88, 90, 167–8, 247, 254
Moslems 20, 68, 72–3, 169

N
Namaste 139–40, 142, 251
Newars 31, 51, 61–5, 77, 108–9, 120, 157, 167, 169, 176, 195–6

O
Office 150, 152, 156, 178–80, 184, 193, 195, 199, 202–4, 223, 251
    hours 206

Culture Shock!

In the same series

Forthcoming